THE INDIAN HEROES

THE INDIAN HEROES

C. A. KINCAID

GYAN

Published by

Gyan Publishing House
5, Ansari Road
Daryaganj, New Delhi-110002
Phone: 011-47034999, 9811692060
E-mail: books@gyanbooks.com

Distribution Network
gyanbooks.com
India, USA, Canada, UK, Australia

ISBN: 978-93-7014-152-0 (PB)

First Published, 1921

2nd Impression 2025

Printed at: Gyan Press, Delhi.

THE INDIAN HEROES
Author: C. A. KINCAID

THE INDIAN HEROES

KING DASHARATHA'S DEATH

THE INDIAN HEROES

BY

C. A. KINCAID, C.V.O.

INDIAN CIVIL SERVICE

AUTHOR OF 'TALES FROM THE INDIAN EPICS,' 'TALES OF THE SAINTS OF PANDHARPUR,' 'A HISTORY OF THE MARATHA PEOPLE,' 'TALES OF KING VIKRAMA' ETC.

FOURTH IMPRESSION

HUMPHREY MILFORD
OXFORD UNIVERSITY PRESS
LONDON NEW YORK TORONTO MELBOURNE
BOMBAY CALCUTTA AND MADRAS
1921

TO MY WIFE

'Now, why have I called this book "The Heroes"? Because that was the name which the Hellenes gave to men who were brave and skilful, and dare do more than other men. At first, I think, that was all it meant: but after a time it came to mean something more; it came to mean men who helped their country; men in those old times, when the country was half-wild, who killed fierce beasts and evil men, and drained swamps, and founded towns, and therefore, after they were dead, were honoured, because they had left their country better than they found it.'

CHARLES KINGSLEY.

CONTENTS

LIST OF ILLUSTRATIONS

PREFACE

IN the following pages I have striven to tell, after the manner of Charles Kingsley, the epic tales of the Indian Heroes. To Anglo-Indians the Ramayana and the Mahabharata are rarely more than mere names. It is my hope that in this little book my fellow officials may read and enjoy a summary of these great poems. To many Indians, of course, the stories of King Rama and of the Bharata Princes are well known. On the other hand, many of my Indian acquaintances have only heard odd bits of these tales in their childhood, and have since entirely forgotten them. The former class will, I trust, be interested to see the heroes of their boyhood portrayed by a Western pen. The latter class may perhaps learn with surprise and pleasure that the epics of their country are as noble as any in the world.

As will be seen from Appendices A, B, and C, I have, at times, departed somewhat widely from the Sanskrit story. I have also on occasion followed popular legend rather than the orthodox text, as in the case of the task required of Draupadi's suitors. The Mahabharata does not relate that the suitors had to aim at the mark, looking only at its reflection in the water. This version is to be found in the folk-tales. And in the Satara Court-house will be found a picture in which this version of the folk-tales is portrayed.

A part of this book has already appeared in the columns of *The Times of India*. I have to thank the Editor for his courtesy in allowing me to reproduce it.

Lastly, my most cordial thanks are due to Mr. H. G. Rawlinson, I.E.S., and to Mr. E. V. Dhayagude for their warm encouragement and their many helpful suggestions.

C. A. K.

NOTE ON THE ILLUSTRATIONS

As the armour and arms and dresses in the illustrations may strike the reader as strange, it is desirable to explain that they have, with the kind assistance of Mr. Bhandarkar of the Bombay Archæological Survey, been copied from the ancient Gandhara sculptures and the bas-relief in the ancient Vihara at Bhaja. These sculptures date from 200 B.C. to A.D. 100, and were therefore more or less contemporaneous with the last recension of the Indian Epics. The heroes and the heroines have been represented as fair men and women of an Aryan type. This is consistent both with Indian tradition and history.

It was hoped at one time that it would be possible to copy the dresses of the women also from ancient Indian patterns. Unfortunately, the garments of the women in the Ajanta paintings, which it was hoped might serve as models, were so scanty and unsuited both to Indian and English taste that the idea had to be abandoned. Instead of the Ajanta paintings, the dresses of the ladies in Mr. Dhurandhar's charming drawings have been followed. In adopting this course it is probable that historical accuracy has not been sacrificed. For the text of the Ramayana and Mahabharata indicates that the dresses of Queen Sita and Draupadi must have been far more elaborate than those of the ladies of Ajanta.

THE INDIAN HEROES

PART I

I

KING DASHARATHA OF AYODHYA

MANY hundred years ago there ruled in Ayodhya a famous king called King Dasharatha, of the noble line of Ikshwaku, of which men said the sun-god himself was the founder. King Dasharatha had three wives, Queens Kausalya, Sumitra, and Kaikeyi. And he had four sons, Rama by Queen Kausalya, Bharata by Queen Kaikeyi, and Laxman and Shatrughna[1] by Queen Sumitra. The four young Princes were beautiful to look upon, and indeed men whispered that the great god Vishnu had divided his divine spirit between them. But of that I know nothing. Only if you had seen them you would have said that they looked like the sons of the Immortals. And Prince Rama was the most beautiful of all the four; indeed, King Dasharatha's subjects loved to call him Ramachandra, or Rama like the Moon, for his face was as fair and bright as a summer moon when it floats in the cloudless skies of India.

[1] The Marathi poet Shridhar, in his Ramavijaya, Adhyaya 4, makes Shatrughna the son of Queen Kaikeyi. But in Valmiki's Ramayana, and in the Raghuvansa, Shatrughna appears as the son of Queen Sumitra. And I have followed the Sanskrit. Tulsidas has also done so.

Now, when King Dasharatha ruled over Ayodhya, the Aryans had only conquered a part of northern India. All the country south of the Ganges was infested by Rakshasas or ogres, and by monsters and cannibals and savages of every kind. And it behoved every young prince to prove his worth by ridding the lands south of the Ganges of the wild beasts and wilder men that dwelt in them. When Prince Rama was only sixteen, a very wise and holy man called Vishvamitra sought the palace and asked for a boon. King Dasharatha inquired what the boon was. Vishvamitra in reply prayed that Prince Rama should be sent back with him, that he might rid the forest in which the sage lived of two demons in human form, called Maricha and Suvahu. They tore to pieces, said the sage, and devoured every man whom they met, and through fear of them Vishvamitra had fled from his hermitage to Ayodhya. King Dasharatha looked sadly at his eldest son, but he knew that the time had come when Rama, as an Aryan Prince, must prove his worth. So the King reluctantly consented. Prince Rama left Ayodhya with Vishvamitra. And with Rama, as his page, there went his favourite brother Prince Laxman.

Ayodhya lay but a day's journey from the Ganges. The Princes and Vishvamitra reached it on the evening of the day on which they left Ayodhya. They halted for the night by the banks of the mighty river, and Vishvamitra lulled the lads to sleep with tales of the saints of old times and of the gods, who in years gone by had visited the holy places of India. Next morning they started once more for Vishvamitra's hermitage. But the path thither led through a forest called the Taraka forest. It was so named because there lived in it Taraka, the mother of the two demons Maricha and Suvahu whom Prince Rama had set out to slay. Now Taraka had guessed that Vishvamitra had fled to Ayodhya in order to seek for aid against her two sons. So she lay in wait in the forest to slay Vishvamitra, as he returned with his helpers. As Prince Rama entered the forest, he twanged his bowstring to see if his bow was ready for use. And no sooner had he done so than Taraka rushed out of the neighbouring thicket. Rama drew his bowstring to his ear and would have shot her with an arrow. But she, seeing the Prince ready, at once made herself invisible. Then, rushing at Rama with a mighty cry, she would have torn him to pieces with her teeth and claws. But the great masters who had taught Prince Rama archery had taught him to shoot by sound as well as by sight, and as the monster rushed at him Rama fired at the spot whence the cry came. So sure was his aim that the arrow pierced Taraka's heart and she fell to earth lifeless.

That night the Princes and Vishvamitra spent in the Taraka forest. And he lulled the boys to sleep with tales of the mighty kings of the Ikshwaku line, from whom they had sprung. And next morning he led them to the hermitage from which he had fled through fear of Taraka's two sons, Maricha and Suvahu. For six days the Princes roamed through the woods, seeking in vain for Vishvamitra's enemies. And on the seventh day, Vishvamitra, thinking that they had fled, offered a sacrifice of thanksgiving to the Immortal Gods. But as he began the celebration, Maricha and Suvahu, who had never left the woods, but had merely hidden themselves as the Princes passed, rushed at them like hawks from the sky, hoping to catch them unawares. But, swiftly though they came, Prince Rama fixed an arrow to his bow more swiftly still. With that arrow he wounded Maricha so sorely that he fell into a neighbouring river and with difficulty escaped to the farther bank. With his second arrow Prince Rama shot Suvahu through the heart. And thus he rid Vishvamitra's forest of the two pests which had haunted it.

Their work finished, Rama and Laxman wished to return to Ayodhya and King Dasharatha. But Vishvamitra told Rama that the time had come for him still further to prove his kingly prowess. Not far from Vishvamitra's hermitage was the kingdom of Mithila. Over it there ruled King Janaka, who had declared that no one should marry his daughter Sita unless he could first bend the mighty bow which the god Shiva had bestowed on King Janaka's ancestor. The beauty of Sita had drawn to Mithila, from far and near, all the young Aryan princes of India. But none had bent the bow; and thus none had carried off to his father's palace the lovely Sita as his bride.

From his hermitage Vishvamitra led Rama and Laxman to Mithila. There King Janaka asked them their business. When he heard that Prince Rama had come as a suitor for the Princess Sita's hand, the King fixed the next day for the trial. All the nobles and people of Mithila assembled at the archery ground, and high above them all, by far the fairest, sat the beautiful Princess Sita. When she saw King Janaka's guards lead Prince Rama into the arena and give him the bow, she prayed to the Immortal Gods that he might bend it and win her for his bride; for such was the boy's beauty and noble bearing that she loved him immediately her eyes met his. And to herself she vowed that, so long as she lived, she never would marry any one but Prince Rama of Ayodhya.

Then Rama took the bow in his left hand and strung it. With his right hand he drew the bow-string taut. But although he pulled with his right hand until the veins stood out on his forehead and the muscles rose up on his back and shoulders the stubborn bow gave not an inch. Princess Sita in despair closed her eyes and prayed to the Immortals who rule the broad heavens to give unto Rama tenfold strength, so that he might bend it and take her for his queen. When again she opened her eyes, she saw the string move slowly outwards until the great back of the bow began to arch and the two points to draw near to each other. And the feathers on the winged arrow came closer and closer to Rama's cheek and the iron head to the wood. And at last when the bow was drawn to its utmost limit there was a noise like a thunder-clap, and down in two pieces at the young hero's feet fell the mighty weapon. King Janaka rose from his throne and proclaimed Prince Rama victorious. And Princess Sita, blushing like a gold mohur-tree in blossom, placed a garland around Rama's neck.

Then King Janaka sent a herald to call King Dasharatha from Ayodhya to Mithila. King Dasharatha came, and with him brought his two other sons, the Princes Bharata and Shatrughna. To Prince Rama, King Janaka gave the Princess Sita. To Prince Laxman, he gave Sita's sister, the Princess Urmila. To the Princes Bharata and Shatrughna, King Janaka gave his two nieces, the Princesses Mándavya and Shrutakirti. With fitting ceremonial and festivities the weddings were celebrated. And thereafter King Dasharatha went back with his sons and their brides to Ayodhya.

The King ruled for several years more over Ayodhya, until at last he began to grow weary beneath the weight of his many winters. He called his counsellors together. He told them that Prince Rama was now in the flower of his age and that it was best that he should become King over Ayodhya and relieve him, King Dasharatha, of the weary burden of power. The counsellors agreed, and the word went forth that on the following day King

Dasharatha would resign his diadem to his son Rama, and that Prince Rama would be crowned King over all the wide lands of Ayodhya. King Dasharatha called Rama to him and told him what had been ordered. And the King gave his son many a wise word of advice, how he should rule over the people entrusted to his care. And all that night Prince Rama and Princess Sita prayed to the Immortals to give the Prince strength and wisdom to rule Ayodhya firmly and justly and well, even as King Dasharatha and all the great house of Ikshwaku had done before him.

But the youngest and fairest of King Dasharatha's three wives was the Queen Kaikeyi, the mother of Prince Bharata. And among her maid-servants was a hump-backed girl called Manthara. When Manthara heard that Prince Rama was to be crowned monarch in King Dasharatha's place, the thought entered her evil mind to excite Queen Kaikeyi to press the claims of Prince Bharata. For if Prince Bharata became King, so the wicked woman thought, she as the favourite maid-servant of the Queen-mother would receive rewards. So Manthara went to Queen Kaikeyi and mocked her and asked how she could listen tamely to the news of Prince Rama's elevation. For the rise of Prince Rama, so Manthara whispered to her mistress, meant first the degradation, and then the imprisonment, and last of all the death, of the other Princes, especially of Prince Bharata. In this way Manthara so worked on Queen Kaikeyi's mind that the Queen vowed that her son Bharata, and Bharata only, should be King of Ayodhya.

Now, in the early days of his reign, King Dasharatha had been grievously wounded while fighting against the wild forest tribes which harassed the borders of his kingdom. Indeed, he would surely have died if Queen Kaikeyi had not nursed him back again to life and health. And in his joy and gratitude he had promised her that, whenever she asked for them, he would grant her two boons, no matter what they were. Through all the intervening years she had never done so. But that very evening she obtained an interview with the aged King. He received her kindly, for he loved her the best of all his wives. And he unfolded to her his plans of resigning the throne to Prince Rama, and told her his hopes that his subjects would enjoy happiness and plenty under their new King.

Queen Kaikeyi listened until he had ceased to speak. Then she cried, 'O King, in years gone by thou didst promise me two boons. For these I have never asked until now. To-day I ask that I be given my reward. My first prayer is that Prince Bharata be crowned King in thy place instead of Prince Rama. My second prayer is that Prince Rama be exiled for fourteen years into the forest.' When King Dasharatha heard Queen Kaikeyi's speech, he made no reply. For he had given his word that whenever she asked for them he would grant Queen Kaikeyi two boons. And the word of an Aryan King could not be broken.

All that night he and Queen Kaikeyi sat silent in King Dasharatha's room. But as the King gave her no answer, Queen Kaikeyi next morning sent for Prince Rama. And she told him how the King had promised her two boons and how he hesitated now to grant them. And she taunted Prince Rama and the King, and asked them whether it was right that an Aryan King should be false to his word. The King bowed his head in silence. But Prince Rama said, 'Thou art right, O Queen. It is not fitting that an Aryan King should be false to his word. Let my brother, therefore, have the kingdom. And to-morrow I shall go away into the forest for fourteen years.' So saying, Prince Rama left the palace and told his mother, Queen Kausalya, and the princess Sita that, in order to keep his father's honour bright, he, Prince Rama, must resign the crown and betake himself as an exile to the wild forests that stretched beyond the kingdom. Queen Kausalya wept bitterly at the news. But the Princess Sita said, 'Nay, the Prince has done well, and I shall go with him into the forests.' And Prince Laxman cried, 'And I, too, shall go with Prince Rama, and I shall serve him as page just as I did when, as boys, we set out with Vishvamitra to the slaying of Taraka and her sons and the winning of Sita.'

Next day, amid the lamentations of all the people, the King's charioteer drove Prince Rama and his wife and brother to the banks of the Ganges, which flowed on the southern boundary of the wide lands of Ayodhya. There Prince Rama dismissed the charioteer and bade him go back. But when King Dasharatha saw the chariot return without either of the Princes or the Princess Sita, he fell suddenly dead of grief in his palace at Ayodhya.

II

THE GOLDEN DEER

AS soon as the death of King Dasharatha became known to his counsellors they met together and resolved, in accordance with the dead King's wishes, to place Prince Bharata on the throne of Ayodhya. Now, at the time when the King sent Prince Rama into exile, Prince Bharata was far away in distant Girivraja, where he and Prince Shatrughna were staying with Queen Kaikeyi's brother, King Kekaya. There the heralds sent by King Dasharatha's counsellors found Prince Bharata. They told him that his father was dead, that Prince Rama was in exile, and that he, as appointed thereto by his father, should return and reign over the wide lands of Ayodhya.

Now Prince Bharata knew nothing of the wickedness of Queen Kaikeyi. And had he been in Ayodhya when she prevailed on King Dasharatha to exile Prince Rama, he, Prince Bharata, would never have suffered it. For he loved Prince Rama as if they two had been full, and not merely half, brothers. When, therefore, Prince Bharata heard the message of the heralds, he grew exceeding wroth. And he vowed that he would find out Prince Rama, wherever he might be, and would force him to return to Ayodhya and rule there. When he reached his father's capital, he stayed there for thirteen days, so that he might perform the last rites over the dead King and so give rest unto his spirit. On the morning of the fourteenth day, he told King Dasharatha's counsellors that never, while Prince Rama lived, would he ascend the throne. And, in spite of their entreaties, he ordered his chariot to be harnessed and, taking with him Prince Shatrughna, he drove away as fast as the swiftest horses in all India could draw his car, and never stayed his course until he saw flashing in the evening sun the waters of the river Ganges, queen of all rivers.

Now after Prince Rama had dismissed his charioteer, he and Prince Laxman and the Princess Sita went to the city of King Guha, who ruled over the Nishadas, and who had in Prince Rama's boyhood been his closest friend. To King Guha, Prince Rama told his story. And the King prayed Prince Rama to stay with him in his capital until the fourteen years of his exile were over. But Prince Rama would not stay. He had promised to spend fourteen years in the forest, and not in the city of his friend. He, therefore, begged King Guha to convey him across the Ganges. And King Guha gave them his own boat, and Rama and Laxman and Sita boarded it. Prince Rama prayed the Ganges to bear them to her southern bank. And the kindly river heard, and her waters bore the boat swiftly to the opposite shore, and there the wanderers entered the wild forests, which were still unsubdued by the Aryan heroes.

On the bank of the Ganges the two Princes and Sita spent the night, and next morning they walked together until they heard the sound of many waters, and they knew that they had reached the spot where the Jumna joins the Ganges. Close by they found a hermitage, in which lived the mighty sage, Bharadwaja. He had crossed to the southern forests, so that he might meditate in peace far from the striving world. Him Prince Rama saluted, and Bharadwaja rose and welcomed the Princes. He prepared a feast in their honour, and that night they rejoiced together. But next morning, when the sun rose, the wise Bharadwaja said, 'Stay here with me, O Prince, until thy fourteen years of exile are over.' But Prince Rama refused. For across the mighty river he could see clearly the cities of the Aryan Princes and he thought that, by staying with the wise Bharadwaja, he would not be carrying out his father's behest.

Then Bharadwaja told him to go, to the Chitrakuta mountain. For it was deep in the forest, and on it was a hermitage where lived saints weary of the world, and with them Prince Rama might live in peace until the days of his exile were over. At Bharadwaja's direction Prince Rama followed the Ganges until he came to the Kalindi river. There they crossed the Kalindi river, and after two days' journey they came to the Chitrakuta mountain. On it Prince Laxman cut down some forest trees, and with their wood he built a hut. And in it Prince Rama and Prince Laxman and the Princess Sita

THE SAGE BHARADWAJA ENTERTAINS THE PRINCES

were living when Prince Bharata went to search for them.

Now when Prince Bharata reached the city of King Guha, he inquired whither Prince Rama had gone. The King of the Nishadas at first feared that Prince Bharata had come to slay his brother. But, learning that he wished merely to escort Prince Rama back to Ayodhya, he gave Prince Bharata a guide and sent him on his way. And at last Prince Bharata came to Prince Rama's hermitage. There he threw himself at his brother's feet and begged his forgiveness. He told him of King Dasharatha's death and how the empty throne of Ayodhya awaited Rama's return. But Prince Rama would not go back with Prince Bharata. For, dead or alive, the word of an Aryan King must not be broken. And for fourteen years he, Rama, would stay in the forest so that the honour of King Dasharatha should be without a stain. At last Prince Bharata agreed to return to Ayodhya, not as King but as his brother's viceroy. When he mounted his chariot, he took with him Prince Rama's sandals. And when he reached Ayodhya he placed the sandals on the throne. And he himself held the royal umbrella over them and fanned them with the royal horse-tails so that men might know that Rama was King of Ayodhya, and that he, Prince Bharata, was but his regent for the fourteen years of his exile.

When Bharata and Shatrughna had returned to Ayodhya, Prince Rama and his brother and wife moved deeper still into the forest. For now that Prince Bharata knew the road to the hermitage, Prince Rama feared that he might again visit him and weary him with entreaties to return to Ayodhya. In this way the exiles came to the forest of Dandaka. Now in the middle of this forest lived a man-eating monster called Viradha. He had once been one of Indra's Gandharvas or singers, and one of the Immortals. But he had cast eyes of love upon Rambha, the fairest dancing girl in Amravati, the god Indra's heaven. And the god Indra punished him for his sin by turning him into a man-eating monster with an elephant's body and a lion's face, but with a man's arms and hands. And he roamed at will through the Dandaka forest.

Now when he saw Prince Rama and his companions, he rose and went to them and said, 'You two men I shall eat, but the woman I shall keep as my wife.' He then seized Sita in his arms and would have carried her away, but Rama shot him in the side with an arrow. At the pain of the wound Viradha dropped Sita. He rushed at Rama and Laxman and lifted one in each arm, meaning to kill them by dashing them to the ground. But the Princes each broke one of the monster's arms and threw him to earth. There they slashed at him with their swords. But they could not kill him, for he was one of the Immortals. So they dug a pit and threw Viradha, still living, into it. And then they covered him up with earth. But Viradha in his agony prayed to the god Indra for forgiveness. And Indra forgave him and freed him from the curse, so that he rose to heaven and once again became an immortal singer in the halls of Amravati.

But the Princes and Princess Sita went ever southward, until they came to the banks of the Godavari. There they met the sage Agastya, who bade them fix their hermitage there. So they built a cottage at Panchavati on the banks of the sacred river, and there they passed the autumn and the winter, with hardly a regret for distant Ayodhya. But one day, as Rama, Laxman, and Sita sat talking by their cottage door, a rakshasi, or demon-woman, called Shurpanakha, passed that way and saw them. Hideous although she was, she fell instantly in love with Prince Rama. And she bade him leave Sita and become her husband. But Prince Rama smilingly mocked Shurpanakha and said, 'Nay, loveliest of women, I am already wedded. Take thou my younger brother, Laxman, as a husband. For his wife is far away.' Then Shurpanakha turned towards Laxman her unsightly face and saw that he, too, was beautiful. So she said, 'So be it; I will take thy brother Laxman as my husband.' But Prince Laxman in turn mocked her and said, 'Nay, O fairest of the fair, I am only a younger brother. Take thou Prince Rama as thy husband, for there is none like him on all the earth.'

Now Shurpanakha did not notice that they mocked her. So she again turned to Rama and said, 'So be it, Prince Rama shall be my husband. But first I shall kill his wife, Sita, for I shall not suffer him to love any one but me.' With these words she rushed at Sita and would have torn her to pieces. But Prince Laxman drew his sword and cut off her ears and nose,[1] and Shurpanakha fled away roaring in agony, until the whole forest resounded with her cries. And she fled away to far Janasthan, where her demon-brothers, Kings Khara and Dushana, dwelt. And she showed them her mutilated face, and she called on them to avenge her upon Rama and Laxman. So Khara and Dushana with their attendants sought out Panchavati, in order to slay Rama and Laxman and Sita. But the Princes guessed that Shurpanakha would seek to be avenged on them. So they ambushed her brothers as they came, and slew them both with arrows; and their attendants fled back to far Janasthan.

Now Shurpanakha had a still mightier brother, called Ravana, who reigned in Lanka or Ceylon,

[1] The town of Nasik, or 'the place of the nose,' is said to derive its name from this incident.

the great island that lies to the south of India. And to him Shurpanakha showed her mutilated face, and called on him to avenge her. But King Ravana feared to share the fate of his brothers Khara and Dushana. So he called to his aid the monster Maricha, whom Prince Rama had wounded while still a boy, near Vishvamitra's hermitage. And their plan of vengeance was this. The monster Maricha was to assume the guise of a wonderful deer with skin that shone like gold, and antlers on which all manner of precious stones glistened. The deer was to draw Rama and Laxman in pursuit of it. And when they had left the hermitage, King Ravana was to seize the Princess Sita and was to sail away with her in the magic car (which years before he had taken by force from Kuber, the god of wealth) until he came to the southern seas and beyond them to Lanka.

So it happened that one day as Prince Rama was about to start on a hunting expedition, the Princess Sita called to him that a deer had strayed close to the hermitage. And as they looked, the deer's hide shone in the sun like pure gold, and its antlers glistened with rubies and emeralds and diamonds. Sita bade her husband shoot it at once, for she longed to have the beautiful hide as a carpet for her cottage and the horns as an ornament for its walls. So Rama took his bow and strove to shoot the deer. But every time he aimed at it, it slipped away behind a forest tree, and in this way it drew him farther and farther from Sita and Laxman. At last Prince Rama was too quick for it, and he shot an arrow that brought it to the ground. But the monster Maricha, although death was nigh, still longed for revenge on Prince Rama. And, imitating Rama's voice, the dying deer called out, 'O Laxman! O Sita!'

The words reached Sita's ears far away in the cottage. And she cried to Laxman, 'Go swiftly after Rama and see what has befallen him.' At first Laxman would not go, for he was loath to leave Sita alone. But the Princess, wild with grief, taunted Laxman with wishing to seize his dead brother's wife. At last Laxman's good sense deserted him, and he left the Princess Sita alone. Following the track of the deer, he at length came to Prince Rama standing near its dead body. They skinned it and brought its hide and flesh and antlers back to their cottage. But when they opened the door, it was empty. Their hearts grew chill within them. They searched everywhere for the Princess, and they roamed through the forest calling to her. But no answer reached their ears except the sound of their own voices, echoed back from the tree-clad hills.

III

PRINCESS SITA'S CAPTIVITY

NOW, ever so high above the earth, King Ravana, like a hawk seeking its prey, was watching Prince Rama's cottage from his magic car. He saw the deer draw Rama away into the woods, and after some little time Laxman follow in their wake. He then descended from the sky. He was hideous to behold, for he had ten heads and twenty arms. And he knew that, if he appeared in this guise, the Princess would flee into the woods and thus escape him. So he changed his shape, and became a holy man wearing a single silken cloth, such as often may still be seen in the towns and on the roads of India. Sita, thinking him to be a harmless mendicant, allowed him to come close to the cottage. When King Ravana had reached the cottage, and the Princess could no longer escape him, he revealed himself to her as the King of the great island of Lanka, girt by the summer seas of the south. The Princess would have none of him and bade him be gone with every angry word that she could think of. But the demon King merely laughed at her. And once more he resumed his hideous form, with its ten heads and twenty arms, and, lifting the Princess by the hair, he bore her away, and threw her into his magic car. Entering it, he first made it soar into the heavens, like an eagle. Then he turned its prow to the southward. And the magic car, like a wild swan at the coming of the northern cold, flew tirelessly towards the southern seas, in which lay Ravana's island kingdom.

Now it so happened that Prince Rama, while living at Panchavati, had made himself beloved by all the beasts and birds of the forest. And a great friendship had grown up between him and the aged King of the vultures, whose name was Jatayu. And as the Princess passed over the woods in the demon King's car, she looked down and saw King Jatayu asleep on one of the trees below her. And she called to him to carry to her husband and Prince Laxman the tidings that the demon King Ravana had borne her away. When King Jatayu heard the Princess's cries, he thought that, in spite of his years, he ought yet to strive to rescue his friend's wife from captivity. So, flying after the magic car, he overtook it and tried to kill King Ravana by tearing him with his claws. But King Ravana drew his sword and cut through the bird King's wings, so that he fell helpless to the ground. And the magic car left the wounded bird far behind as it sped towards the southern seas. As the car passed over a hill, the Princess looked down and saw a band of monkeys seated on it. Prompted by despair, she flung down to them her scarf and her jewellery, in the hope that, somehow or other, they might convey the news of her fate to Prince Rama of Ayodhya. But the magic car bore her away until below her she saw the southern ocean and then the great island of Lanka. In a few moments more, the car alighted, and King Ravana lodged his captive securely within the walls of his palace.

In the meantime the two Princes continued their search for the lost Princess, until, at last, they reached the place where King Jatayu had tried in vain to rescue the captive Sita. They saw the bird King lying helplessly on the ground, with his wings cut through, and near to death. Yet he greeted his friend Prince Rama and told him that it was King Ravana who had carried away the Prince's wife. But he died before he could tell the distracted Prince the country of King Ravana or the direction of his flight. Thus the Princes continued their search until they entered the Krauncha forest. There suddenly they heard a mighty roar and at the same moment two huge hands shot forth and each hand seized one of the brothers. They looked up and saw that a headless giant called Kavandha had caught them and was about to tear them in pieces and devour them through his mouth, which he had open in his belly. Prince Rama, overcome with grief, would have welcomed death. But Laxman exhorted him to play the man. And they drew their swords and slashed at Kavandha's arms until they dropped off and the demon fell swooning to the ground. They then piled firewood about him and set fire to it. And the flames soon spread to Kavandha's body and reduced it to ashes.

Now Kavandha had, in the pride of his youth, challenged the god Indra to mortal combat. And Indra had hurled him to the ground with a single thunderbolt. Then, pitying his fallen state, he had promised him immortality on the day that Prince Rama should slay him. So when, purified by the fire, Kavandha's spirit rose to Indra's heaven, it called, deeply grateful for its release from its monstrous body, to Prince Rama to go southward, until he came to the Matanga hill, at the foot of which lay the Pampa lake.

Now it so chanced that the Matanga hill was the hill where the Princess Sita had, as she passed over it, cast down her scarf and jewellery. And the monkeys whom she had seen were no ordinary monkeys. They were a band of exiles, and their leader was the monkey Prince Sugriva, whom his elder brother, King Vali, had driven from the kingdom of Kishkindha and robbed of his Princess. When the exiles saw the Princes Rama and Laxman near their hiding-place, they sent a messenger to learn their business. For they feared that the two brothers were spies sent by King Vali, so that he might track them out and destroy them. But Prince Rama told the herald that he was but the exiled Prince of Ayodhya, who searched for his wife, the lovely Princess Sita. So the herald took the brothers into the presence of the monkey Prince Sugriva.

After Sugriva had heard their story, he fetched from a cavern in the hill the scarf and ornaments which Sita had thrown to earth as King Ravana bore her away. When Rama and Laxman saw them they knew them at once and vowed that they would be revenged upon the wicked King who had robbed Prince Rama of his bride. But Sugriva did his best to console them, and he told them that he, too, had lost his bride. And Rama, finding that they were both exiles, warmed towards the monkey Prince and promised to help him to regain Kishkindha if Sugriva would afterwards help him in the quest for Sita. As he made the offer he shot an arrow at a neighbouring tree. And the arrow passed through the tree and through six others beyond. Seeing Rama's incomparable skill as an archer, Sugriva greeted him as an ally and vowed that, if he ever won back Kishkindha, he, Sugriva, would not rest until he had reunited Sita and Rama.

So the Princes and the exiles went south, until they came to Kishkindha. When they approached its high walls, the sentries told King Vali that a hostile band was nearing his capital, and King Vali gathered his soldiers. And as they were far more numerous than Sugriva's band, the exiles would soon have been overpowered. But Prince Rama drew his bow and shot an arrow that pierced King Vali to the heart. When his soldiers saw their King fall, they fled in dismay, and the monkey Prince Sugriva, with Rama and Laxman, entered Kishkindha in triumph, and they crowned Sugriva King of all the wide lands of his fathers.

But it was now the rainy season and the forests were overgrown with creepers. The streams were swollen to rivers and the rivers to seas. So King Sugriva bade Prince Rama wait until autumn had passed before they went forth to seek where King Ravana had hidden Sita. But when autumn came, King Sugriva forgot all about his promise to Rama. And the latter waited vainly. At last in despair he sent Laxman to King Sugriva, and Prince Laxman reminded the King of his promise. Then King Sugriva's conscience smote him and he sent forth his heralds and he called together his armies. When his warriors had assembled he bade them go forth, north and south and east and west, so that they might learn whither King Ravana had borne away Sita.

And over the force that went southward King Sugriva placed King Vali's son, Prince Angada, whom he had adopted as his own child. When Prince Angada came to the shores of the southern ocean, he met an aged vulture called Sampati, the elder brother of King Jatayu, who had striven to free the Princess Sita from the wicked King Ravana. In olden days, Sampati and Jatayu had, in the pride of their youth, vowed that they would fly into the sun. And the sun-god in his wrath had tried to smite them dead with his rays. But Sampati had shielded his brother Jatayu. So the latter had escaped and lived to be King over all the vultures. But the sun-god's rays had burnt up Sampati's wings. So he had fallen by the sea-shore, and had lived there miserably ever since. When the monkey army under Prince Angada told Sampati that they sought the Princess Sita, he answered them that he had seen, passing high over his head, King Ravana's magic car on the way to Lanka, and that in the car there was a lovely woman, who wept as the King bore her away. So Prince Angada learnt that the demon King had not hidden Sita anywhere in India, but had borne her across the seas to his mighty island of Lanka.

Now among the army led by Prince Angada was a famous warrior called Maruti. His mother, Anjani, was the wife of one Kesarin. But as she wandered, alone among the hills, the wind-god Maruti saw and loved her, and Maruti was their son. And his father gave him as his birthright the power to rise, even as he, the wind-god, did, into the skies, and to fly over the earth and the mountains and the ocean. So when the aged vulture Sampati told Prince Angada that Sita had been borne away to Lanka, Maruti said that he would leap across the ocean and seek her out. As he spoke, Maruti rose from the shore of India, and the monkey army watched him as he soared high above the ocean and disappeared into the southern sky. At last Maruti alighted on the mountain peaks of the great southern island, and there he saw spread far and wide below him the mighty city of Lanka. From the mountain peaks, Maruti bounded on to the roof of the palace of the King. But, though he peered in at every window, he could see no one whom he recognized as the lady who had thrown at his feet her scarf and jewels from the magic car.

Now King Ravana had at first taken the captive Princess to his palace, and there he had tried often and often to win her for his bride. But the Princess, prisoner though she was, would not, while life endured, be faithless to the gallant husband who had won her on the archery ground of Mithila. So King Ravana grew wroth and banished her from his city, and sent her, with demon women to guard her, to a forest, called the Asoka forest, wherein stood his summer palace.

And Maruti, after searching in vain for Princess Sita through all Lanka, cast his eyes round the horizon, and he saw in the distance King Ravana's summer palace. From Lanka's walls a single bound carried Maruti to the Asoka forest. There he climbed into a tree and looked through the palace gardens. At last in one corner of a close he saw a lady weeping by herself. Her clothes were torn and soiled. Around her was a band of hideous guards, who continually mocked the weeping woman. And they bade her lay aside her pride and gratefully welcome as her husband the mighty Ravana, who was King of all the land. But the weeping woman merely shook her head. And then she lifted her face and looked at them in scorn. As she did so, Maruti saw before him the loveliest face in all the world, the face of the lady who had thrown down the scarf and jewels from the flying car. And Maruti knew that his quest was over and that the lady whom he saw was the Princess Sita.

PRINCESS SITA IN CAPTIVITY

IV

THE FINDING OF SITA

WHEN Maruti knew that he had found the Princess Sita, he was at a loss how to attract her attention without being perceived by the demon women who guarded her. But after a time they ceased to mock her and, throwing themselves on the ground, fell asleep. Then Maruti, from his station in the tree above Sita, began to tell, in a sweet voice and low, the wondrous deeds of Prince Rama, how he slew Taraka and her son Suvahu, how he snapped in twain the mighty bow which the god Shiva had given to King Janaka's ancestor, and how, to keep bright his father's honour, he resigned the crown of Ayodhya and went as an exile into the southern forests.

And as Sita listened to the tale, her eyes roamed from tree to tree, and at last they fell on Maruti hidden above her. At first, she thought that King Ravana had come to mock at her in a monkey's guise. But Maruti told her that he was Prince Rama's friend and showed her a signet ring which the Prince had given him, when he first went forth on the quest of Sita. When Sita saw the ring, her hopes rose high within her, and she told Maruti all the evil that had befallen her, how King Ravana had by a trick borne her away, and how, to punish her, because she scorned his wooing, he had imprisoned her in his palace in the Asoka forest. In exchange for Prince Rama's ring she gave Maruti her jewelled tiara, that he might cheer her lover by the sight of it. And Maruti took it and thought of returning to India.

Then he looked around him, and his heart filled with wrath because of the cruel prison in which Sita lay. He pressed her to come with him, and promised that he would carry her back safely over the southern ocean. But she refused. For she said that no one should hold her in his arms with her consent except Prince Rama. Then the wind-god's son thought that he would leave behind him some trace that a son of the Immortals had been to the Asoka forest. So he began to pull up the trees all round the palace and to make of its fair gardens a wilderness. Now it so happened that a body of Ravana's guards under his captain, Jambu-mali, were passing by, and when they saw the destruction which Maruti had wrought they rushed to seize him. And Jambu-mali and Maruti fought a deadly fight in King Ravana's pleasure-ground. But brave though Jambu-mali was, he could not overcome a son of the Immortals. Maruti shattered Jambu-mali's head with the trunk of a mighty tree, and he fell lifeless to the ground.

But the noise of the struggle had drawn more and more troops to the Asoka forest, and at last Maruti was taken captive and brought into the presence of King Ravana. The demon King ordered him to be taken outside and executed. But he pleaded that he had come as an envoy of Prince Rama. And King Ravana's brother, the good Prince Vibhishan, begged for Maruti's life. 'For,' said the good Prince, 'an envoy's life is sacred.' Then the cruel demon King laughed and said, 'My brother, at thy wish I spare his life. But he shall not go back unpunished.' So he ordered his guards to tie cloth, soaked in oil, round Maruti's tail and then to set it alight. And this was done. But Maruti, maddened by the pain, broke loose from his tormentors and, bounding on to the roof of the palace, fled toward the sea-shore. As he fled the burning cloth fell from his tail and set fire to the demon King's dwelling-place and all the fair city of Lanka. Maruti heard behind him, as he sprang back to India, the roaring of the flames as they ate up

Lanka city. And when he alighted on the southern ocean's farther shore, he could still see the southern sky, red with the flames of the burning town. Then he told Prince Angada that he had seen Sita. And right glad were the Prince and his army to hear the news. For now they could cease from their quest and return to Kishkindha.

When they came to the city of King Sugriva, Maruti told him and Rama and Laxman his story, and the two brothers wept for joy at the tale. King Sugriva ordered his hosts to assemble next day, and, marching directly south, they reached in due course the shores of the southern ocean. But here despair overtook Prince Rama. For in all the army of King Sugriva there was only Maruti, the son of the wind-god, who could spring across the waves to Lanka. So the Prince wandered in grief and rage by the shore until Varuna, the god of the ocean, took pity on him. And, as Prince Rama sat looking at the waves, he became aware that a kingly figure stood in front of him. And this kingly figure said, 'I am the god of ocean, and I have come to help thee to cross the waves to Lanka. In the army of King Sugriva there is one Nala, the son Vishvakarma, the artificer of the gods; and if he build a bridge to Lanka, I, the ocean god, will bear it up.'

With these words the figure vanished, and Prince Rama saw his visitor no more. But he took the message of the ocean god to King Sugriva, who ordered Nala to build the bridge. Then all the host hurled stones and trees into the sea. And the kindly ocean god bore up the bridge upon his breast, so that it soon stretched far away to the great southern island. When the bridge was finished, King Sugriva and his army, and Prince Rama and his brother crossed it dry-foot and marched towards the fair city of Lanka.

PRINCE RAMA AND THE GOD OF OCEAN

Now it so happened that, before King Sugriva's army had bridged the southern ocean, the good and wise Prince Vibhishan had strongly pressed his brother, King Ravana, to save himself and Lanka from their fate, by restoring the Princess Sita to her grieving husband. But the wicked King upbraided his brother so sharply, that the good and wise Prince Vibhishan left King Ravana and his island to their evil destiny, and crossing to the southern shore of India, declared himself an ally of King Sugriva, and Prince Rama. And after King Sugriva's army had crossed to Lanka, Prince Vibhishan showed them the roads that led to the city.

All round Lanka, King Sugriva's army camped, and everywhere King Ravana's warriors went outside the walls to do battle with King Sugriva's soldiers. Fierce was the fighting and many warriors fell on both sides. But the fighting was fiercest close to the northern gate. For there were stationed Prince Rama and Prince Laxman. And, in their longing to recover the Princess, they fought like men possessed. Indeed, they would soon have swept away all the warriors opposed to them, had King Ravana not posted opposite the Princes the pick of his fighting men and encouraged them with his own presence and example.

Thus for many a weary year the fighting lasted, until King Ravana's mightiest warriors had one by one fallen outside the gates of Lanka. At last the King's bravest son, the Prince Indrajit, asked leave to go forth and do battle with the Princes of Ayodhya. King Ravana's heart sank within him, for of all his sons Prince Indrajit was the one whom he loved the most. Nevertheless he gave Indrajit leave to go forth and win, if he could, immortal renown.

When Prince Indrajit had left behind him the walled city of Lanka and had drawn near to where

Princes Rama and Laxman were fighting against the demon King's armies, Prince Indrajit, through the magic power inherited by him from his father, made himself invisible. And, soaring high into the heavens, he shot shaft after shaft at Rama and Laxman. Look where they would, they could see nothing but the arrows, which seemed to come towards them from every quarter of the sky. And, at last, overcome with wounds, the two brothers fainted and fell motionless to earth. Prince Indrajit strode back in triumph to his father's palace and boasted that he had slain King Ravana's foes.

The King, overjoyed, embraced the Prince, and taking his magic car flew in it to his summer palace in the Asoka forest. There he seized the lovely Princess Sita and, throwing her weeping into his car, he drove her through the air high over the battlefield. Mocking at her, he pointed out to her the forms of her husband and his brother, where they lay as still as did the bodies of the dead warriors around them. And King Ravana asked her in bitter jest, if she still thought that Prince Rama would rescue her from captivity and take her back to be Queen over the wide lands of Ayodhya. The Princess Sita said nothing, but wept in bitter sorrow. At last King Ravana, weary of his cruel sport, took her back in his car to the summer palace, where he held her captive. But in King Sugriva's army there was nothing but sorrow and dismay. For the Princes were the bravest of all the brave men there. It was, moreover, to recover the Princess for her husband that King Sugriva had set forth. If her husband were dead, there remained no longer any cause for the war.

Now there was an ancient counsellor of King Sugriva called Sushena. And he spoke to King Sugriva and bade him be of good courage. 'There is,' said Sushena, 'far beyond the course of any mariner an ocean called the Milky Ocean, and there the god Vishnu has his throne. In the Milky Ocean there is an island, which bears on its heart two mountains, called Chandra and Drona. On those mountains grows the herb Vishalya from which the gods make ambrosia, and which can restore the wounded to health and the dead to life. If any of the King's messengers can bring the Vishalya herb here from the Milky Ocean, life will at once return to the Princes of Ayodhya.'

When King Sugriva's warriors heard that the herb lay in an island in the Milky Ocean, their hearts sank within them, for there was none among them who dared to venture on such a journey. But Maruti, the son of the wind-god, rose in his place and said, 'O King, I will fetch the herb Vishalya from the mountains Drona and Chandra.' And he sprang up far into the west, and flew on until he became a speck in the sky and then vanished. He kept his course due westward, until he saw the ocean become whiter and whiter. At last it turned to milk, and then he knew that he had reached the Milky Ocean, where the god Vishnu has his throne. At length he saw an island with two hills upon it, and he knew that he had ended his quest. He landed on the island and plucked, from the sides of the hills, handfuls of the healing herb, Vishalya. And the touch of the herb made his hands and face shine with health and strength. Then once again he sprang into the air. Soon King Sugriva's warriors watching the western sky saw a speck which grew larger every moment till at last they saw the son of the wind-god coming faster and faster towards them. When he alighted near King Sugriva's camp, he showed the King the healing herb. And Sushena took it and applied it first to Rama and then to Laxman. And their wounds healed forthwith and they came back to life again with greater strength than they had possessed before. A great shout went up from King Sugriva's host. And King Ravana's spies told him that the Princes had risen from the dead.

When Prince Indrajit heard this, he again took leave of his father to go forth and do battle with the sons of King Dasharatha. And again the Prince Indrajit made himself invisible, and again he began to shower arrows on Prince Rama and Prince Laxman, without their knowing where to shoot back. But this time the good and wise Prince Vibhishan was near Prince Rama. He knew the secret of Prince Indrajit's magic, and his eyes could pierce the veil of cloud with which Prince Indrajit hid himself from King Sugriva's warriors. He showed to Prince Laxman the spot where to shoot. And Laxman, drawing his bowstring to his ear, shot an arrow at Indrajit, that entered between the joint of his helmet and his breastplate. And as the arrow pierced the joint of his armour, King Ravana's bravest son fell lifeless to the ground.

When the King heard the news of his son's death, he realized that nothing remained for him but to die in battle at the head of his army. Prince Rama saw King Ravana advance from Lanka, and he stepped forward in front of the warriors of King Sugriva and challenged the wicked King to mortal combat. King Ravana joyfully accepted the challenge; and in the sight of the two armies the Prince and the King fought to the death for the hand of the Princess Sita. For a long time neither the King nor the Prince prevailed in the fight. But at last Prince Rama prayed to the sun-god, from whose loins his race, so men said, was sprung. And as Prince Rama prayed, he fitted an arrow to his bow and drew the bow until the points met. The arrow pierced King Ravana's golden breastplate and clove his heart in twain, and the wicked King fell headlong from his chariot and lay dead on the ground, his ten heads covered with blood and dust. When they saw King Ravana dead, his warriors fled from the field back to the city. And King Sugriva and the Princes entered the gates and seated the good and wise Prince Vibhishan on the throne of Lanka.

Then Prince Rama searched for Princess Sita, until he found her captive in the summer palace in the Asoka forest. But when the Prince saw her in the palace of the wicked King, all his love for her vanished and a cruel jealousy took its place. And he upbraided her as unfaithful to her husband, and bade her go where she would, as he would no longer honour her as his wife. When Princess Sita heard this, she felt that, without Prince Rama's love, life was a worthless possession. So she sent for Prince Laxman and bade him get ready a funeral pyre. And Prince Laxman built the pyre high of wood from the Asoka forest. And when it was finished, he poured oil on it. The Princess took a torch in her hand, and with firm wrist lit the pyre. Then, making obeisance to her husband, and walking round him as a worshipper walks round the shrine of a god, the Princess passed straight into the roaring flames.

V

THE RETURN TO AYODHYA

WHEN Prince Rama saw the Princess Sita enter the burning pyre, he yearned to call her to him, but again jealousy blazed up in his heart and kept him from uttering the words that rose to his lips. But when the fire had consumed her, and he realized that the bride of his youth had gone, his jealousy went, and grief unbearable took its place. Back to his mind flashed their first meeting when he was a boy at Mithila, her blushing smiles when she flung round his neck the garland that was to bind them for ever, the happy years together in Ayodhya, her refusal to leave him when exiled, their months of hardship on the banks of the Godavari, and then the weary quest for her that now had ended fruitlessly. And he wept so long and bitterly that the Immortals had pity on him, and they persuaded the fire-god to give back Sita to Prince Rama. And as he looked at the ashes of the pyre, he suddenly saw rise from them the lovely form of the bride of his boyhood. Her eyes looked at him with unquenchable love, and the smile on her lips told him that she forgave him everything. And once again husband and wife embraced each other, just as they had done in the palace of Ayodhya.

Then Prince Rama went to the wise and good King Vibhishan of Lanka and told him that he must return to Ayodhya. For the fourteen years of exile had passed, King Dasharatha's honour was untarnished, and Prince Rama was free to claim the inheritance of the great house of Ikshwaku. King Vibhishan offered him the magic car in which King Ravana had borne away his lovely captive. And Prince Rama begged both King Vibhishan and King Sugriva with their warriors and courtiers to return with him to the city of Ayodhya. They eagerly agreed to go with Prince Rama, and so huge was the magic car that all found ample room in it. That it might the better bear their weight, King Vibhishan harnessed to the car twelve wild swans. And, helped by their mighty wings, the magic car rose into the heavens.

Then it bore its load to the northward, where lay the wide lands and the walled cities of Ayodhya. Beneath them they could see the southern ocean dashing against the bridge with which Vishvakarma's son Nala had spanned it. Then they passed over the southern forests. And Prince Rama, as they went, pointed out to the Princess the spot where Prince Angada had found the vulture Sampati, and King Sugriva's city Kishkindha, and the place where Prince Rama and Prince Laxman had met the gallant bird King, Jatayu. Then, in turn, Princess Sita pointed out to Prince Rama the hermitage where they had spent so many long hours. And the eyes of both filled with tears as they gazed.

And they passed over the forests of Dandaka and Taraka, until at last they came near the capital of King Guha, the friend of Prince Rama's boyhood. There Prince Rama brought the magic car to earth. For he wished to learn how Prince Bharata had borne himself during the fourteen years of exile. Prince Rama called Maruti to him, and he bade the wind-god's son go to Ayodhya and learn whether Prince Bharata had kept his faith, or whether he had had himself crowned King of Ayodhya. The wind-god's son sprang high into the heavens, and his leap carried him to within a mile of Ayodhya. Close to where he alighted he saw a hermitage. Inside it he saw an anchorite, clad in a wild deer's skin and doing obeisance to a pair of sandals. Then Maruti knew that Prince Bharata had kept faith with his brother. Maruti approached Prince Bharata and did obeisance to him and said, 'O Prince, the fourteen years of thy brother Prince Rama's exile are passed. And he has come to the country of the Nishadas, and he has sent me to tell thee, O Prince, of his coming.'

Then Prince Bharata fell on Maruti's neck and wept for joy, and he showered gifts on the son of the wind-god in return for his joyful tidings. And Prince Bharata bade Maruti take him to King Guha's court that he might without delay do obeisance to his brother. Maruti led Prince Bharata to the country of the Nishadas, and Prince Bharata went clothed in scanty rags, and had borne in front of him the sandals which his elder brother had given him fourteen years before.

When Prince Bharata came close to Prince Rama, he threw himself at Rama's feet and resigned to him the glory and the burden of the kingship of Ayodhya. Then they all ascended the magic car and, helped by the twelve wild swans, the magic car bore them to Ayodhya. The next day Prince Rama was crowned King, in King Dasharatha's place. And the splendour of the crowning far surpassed the crownings of any of the mighty line of the house of Ikshwaku. But as the days passed, King Sugriva and King Vibhishan began to think of Kishkindha and Lanka. And they took leave of King Rama, and the car bore them back again to their southern homes, and then returned to Ayodhya, that it might accomplish the wishes of King Rama. But King Rama bade it go back to Kuber, the god of wealth. And, drawn by the wild swans, the magic car rose into the heavens and vanished.

For many months after Kings Sugriva and Vibhishan had left Ayodhya, King Rama and his Queen Sita lived together in great happiness. But one day King Rama sent for one of his counsellors, Vadra by name, and bade him repeat what his subjects said among themselves about him and Queen Sita. Then Vadra said, 'Thy subjects, O King, praise thy valour and thy virtues greatly. But they wonder how thou didst come to take Queen Sita back to thy arms after she had spent so many years in the palace of King Ravana.' On hearing these words all King Rama's jealousy blazed up again within his heart, and he sent for his brother, Prince Laxman. And King Rama bade Prince Laxman take Queen Sita into the forests that lay beyond his kingdom to the south of the Ganges river and leave her there.

Then Prince Laxman with a heavy heart ordered the charioteer, Sumantra, to yoke swift steeds to the royal chariot, and in it Prince Laxman drove to Queen Sita's palace. There he prayed Queen Sita to come with him on a pilgrimage to the hermitage of the sage Valmiki, who lived in the forests that stretched beyond the kingdom to the south of the river Ganges.

The good Queen Sita trusted Prince Laxman and mounted the chariot, which King Rama's swift steeds drew in a few hours to the banks of the mighty river. On reaching the northern bank, Prince Laxman took Queen Sita in a boat, and the flood bore them to the southern bank. When they had reached it, Queen Sita stepped ashore, but Prince Laxman did not follow her. Remaining in the boat, he begged her forgiveness. Then he told her that King Rama had renounced her and had exiled her to the forests beyond the Ganges. Queen Sita fainted and fell to earth, and Prince Laxman, with a heavy heart and weeping eyes, ordered his rowers to row him to the northern shore. There he mounted his chariot and in it returned to the palace at Ayodhya.

When Queen Sita returned to consciousness, she could but just see Prince Laxman's boat nearing the northern bank of the Ganges river. She was too proud to call him back to her, for Prince Laxman, as she knew, had but obeyed the orders of King Rama, her husband. So she rose and walked sadly into the forest until she came to a hermitage in a lonely glade. In the hermitage lived the sage Valmiki, a wise and holy man, whom King Dasharatha had known and honoured. When she saw the sage Valmiki, she humbly touched his feet. He raised the Queen and welcomed her, and gave her to the care of some female anchorites who lived close by. And some months later she gave birth to twin sons. The sage Valmiki gave to one the name of Kusha and to the other the name of Lava. For in order to guard them from evil spirits he rubbed the body of one with Kusha, or the upper part of the grass stalks, and that of the other with Lava, or the lower part of the grass stalks, which grew near his hermitage.

Now, when some years had passed, King Rama, who had conquered or levied tribute from all the countries around Ayodhya, announced that he would hold an *Aswamedha* or horse-sacrifice. All the kings of India from the Himalayas to the island of Lanka sent him gifts and tribute. And King Rama gave a mighty feast and scattered gold and jewels among his guests. When the feast was well-nigh over, a herald brought the King word that two boy singers were without, and that, if the King granted them leave, they would sing a song that would please his guests. The King nodded his head in assent, and the herald brought the two boys in. They were tall and strong, and their faces shone so fair and bright: that each guest turned to his neighbour and asked, 'Who can these boys be? For verily they bear themselves like the sons of the immortals.'

But the boys tuned their instruments, and then in low, sweet voices began to sing of the boyhood of King Rama, and how he slew Taraka and Suvahu, how he wooed and won the Princess Sita, and how to save his father's honour he resigned his crown for fourteen years. And the guests looked one at the other, for they marvelled how the boys could have learned what had happened so long ago. And then the song began to tell how the evil King Ravana had carried off the lovely Sita, and how the Princes Rama and Laxman had searched for her, mourning through the lonely forest. And the voices of the singers were so full of feeling, that the tears rolled down the cheeks of King Rama and his assembled guests as they listened. Then the boys began to sing of the march on Lanka and the fights between Laxman and Indrajit, between King Rama and Ravana. And their voices rose until they sounded like the pealing of a mighty organ. And the rafters gave back the sound until King Rama and his guests saw, as if in a vision, the far off walls of King Ravana's city, and longed to be there again and to fight once more with the hosts of the demon King.

At last King Rama cried, 'Who, fair sirs, are ye, who sing of my past life with voices like the Gandharvas of Amravati?' And the boys threw themselves at the King's feet and told him that they were the two sons, Lava and Kusha, whom Queen Sita had borne to the King in Valmiki's hermitage; and that the sage had written the song and had made them learn it, and had then sent them to sing it at the horse-sacrifice of King Rama. The heart of King Rama was touched, and he bade his charioteer bring him again Queen Sita from the hermitage. But after the charioteer had left, the King's jealousy again seized him. And he thought to himself, 'Even though Queen Sita remained pure in King Ravana's palace, how do I know that she remained pure in Valmiki's hermitage?' So when his charioteer drove Queen Sita back to Ayodhya, King Rama bade her swear in the presence of his guests that she had remained pure not only in Lanka but in the forest glade.

Then Queen Sita felt that, while she lived, King Rama would never cast aside his doubts. So in a firm voice she called aloud, 'O Mother Earth, if I am pure, if I have never in thought, word, or deed loved any one but King Rama, do thou take me now to thy bosom.' Then from the earth there rose a golden throne, and on it the Queen Sita seated herself. Directly she seated herself the kindly earth took back the throne with Queen Sita on it to her bosom, and on the spot where she had been there lay but a garland of flowers. Again King Rama was torn with grief, and he prayed once more to the Immortal Gods to give him back Queen Sita. But this time the Immortals pitied him not. There came to him a voice from heaven saying, 'Sita has ascended to heaven, and there only shalt thou meet her.'

So King Rama turned his thoughts to his kingdom and his conquests, and for many years he ruled them wisely and well. Then Prince Laxman died. And the King's sorrow for his brother and his Queen became more than he could bear. He called to him his brothers, his sons, and his nephews. To Prince Bharata the King offered the throne of Ayodhya, over which he had ruled as regent so long and so justly. But Prince Bharata said, 'Where thou goest, O King, I go. Divide, therefore, thy kingdom between thy two sons Kusha and Lava.' So King Rama gave to Kusha the southern half and to Lava the northern half of his kingdom. Then King Rama would have made Prince Shatrughna King over the lands of Mathura, which he had conquered for King Rama from a wicked ruler called Lavana. But Prince Shatrughna said, just as Prince Bharata had said, 'O King, where thou goest, I go.' So King Rama divided the kingdom of Mathura between Prince Shatrughna's two sons, Suvahu and Shatrughati.

Then, followed by a great multitude, King Rama and his brothers made their way to the banks of the Saraju river, and to its kindly waters they resigned their weary frames. And, while the multitude sorrowed for their dead King, they saw the magic car which had brought him and Queen Sita back from Lanka descend slowly from the skies.

QUEEN SITA MEETS KING RAMA IN HEAVEN

And to meet it there rose from the surface of the waters the spirit forms of King Rama and his two brothers. The car bore them swiftly upwards until the watchers saw it mount to Vaikunth, the god Vishnu's heaven. They saw the portals open wide, and then they saw Queen Sita with a smile of infinite joy and forgiveness on her lips stand in the open doorway and with loving arms clasp King Rama to her bosom.

PART II

VI

THE PRINCES OF ELEPHANT CITY

MANY years after King Rama and Queen Sita had been united for ever in Vishnu's heaven, there ruled another great line of Aryan Princes in Northern India. Just as the house of Rama was known as the line of Ikshwaku, so the other house was known as the line of Bharata. For King Bharata was one of the founders of its glory. And just as the house of Ikshwaku claimed to be sprung from the loins of the sun-god, so the Bharatas boasted their descent from the loins of the moon-god. The town in which the Bharatas ruled was known as Hastinapura and was about sixty miles from the city which to-day men call Delhi. Now Hastinapura, being interpreted, is the Elephant City. And men came to call it so because of the hundreds of war elephants that guarded the throne of the Bharatas and the wide lands over which they ruled. So great and warlike, indeed, was the Bharata house that it has given its name to India, which even to-day is called the Bharatvarsha, or the land of the Bharatas. And the greatest poem in all the world is called the Mahabharata, because it tells of the wars and the loves of the Bharata Princes.

Now King Vichitravirya was the great-great-grand-son of the King Bharata from whom the line of the Bharatas took their name. But King Vichitravirya died of a decline in the flower of his age. He left behind him two widows, who bore him after his death two sons, by name Dhritarashtra and Pandu. Dhritarashtra was the elder, but as he was born blind, his brother Pandu became

King over Hastinapura. King Pandu's wife, Queen Kunti, bore him three sons, Yudhishthira, Bhima, and Arjuna. And his Queen Madri bore him two sons, Nakula and Sahadev. But Pandu died young far away among the peaks of the Himalayas, and his brother Dhritarashtra, in spite of his blindness, succeeded him as King over the empire of the Bharatas. Queen Madri burned herself on the funeral pyre with her dead lord, for he had loved her very dearly. Queen Kunti took King Pandu's five sons and returned with them to Hastinapura, where King Dhritarashtra welcomed them as if they had been his own children. And in the royal palace the sons of King Pandu played and learned and grew up together with one hundred sons whom his Queen Gandhari had borne to King Dhritarashtra. But the sons of King Pandu became tall and strong and beautiful as are the Immortals. And men whispered that King Pandu was not their true sire, but that Prince Yudhishthira's father was Dharma, the god of justice, that Prince Bhima's father was Wayu, god of the winds, that Prince Arjuna's father was the god Indra, who rules over the broad sky, and that the fathers of Nakula and Sahadev were the Ashwins, the two divine stars that may be seen at night shining high up in the eastern heavens.

Now King Dhritarashtra appointed one Drona to teach his sons and nephews the use of arms. He was the son of the sage Bharadwaja, and he had no equal as archer and man-at-arms in all the lands of the Aryans. Under his guidance the young Princes became skilled in the use of the Aryan weapons. But the sons of King Pandu far surpassed in skill the sons of King Dhritarashtra. Prince Yudhishthira, who was the wisest as well as the eldest of the princes, became the most daring charioteer in all Northern India; Bhima became the most cunning

THE WAR ELEPHANTS OF HASTINAPURA

with the mace; Prince Arjuna the surest archer; and Princes Nakula and Sahadev the best swordsmen among all the warriors of that day. And in the heart of King Dhritarashtra's eldest son, the Prince Duryodhan, there grew up a bitter jealousy of his cousins and especially of Prince Bhima. For not only in mace-play, but in boxing, wrestling, and running, Prince Bhima had no equal among the Aryan nobles.

When the royal princes were nearing manhood, their teacher, Drona, the son of Bharadwaja, obtained leave of King Dhritarashtra to prove to the world the prowess of his pupils. Now Drona had a bitter foe, one Drupada, the King of the Panchalas, for when Drona was poor King Drupada had scorned his friendship. So Drona led the royal princes against the country of the Panchalas. And before the blows of Prince Bhima's mace, the arrows of Prince Arjuna, and the deadly sword-thrusts of the Princes Nakula and Sahadev, the warriors of King Drupada went down like corn before the sickle. At last Prince Arjuna took King Drupada captive and led him before Drona. Drona gave King Drupada his life, but to punish him for his scorn in days gone by, Drona took from him half his kingdom.

King Drupada returned to Panchala; but in his heart there grew up fierce anger against the Bharata Princes. For without their aid Drona would never have come by his revenge. So when the King reached his palace grounds, he made a mighty sacrifice to the Immortals who rule the broad heavens. And at the time of the sacrifice he prayed with all his heart to them that they would create something which would destroy utterly the line of the Bharatas. And the Immortal Gods were gladdened at the sacrifice and listened kindly to King Drupada's prayer. And lo! as the flames died down on the sacrificial fire, King Drupada saw sitting where the flames had been a young girl of wondrous beauty. At the same time he heard a voice in the heavens that said, 'She will be the best of women, yet will she come to be the ruin of the house of the Bharatas.' King Drupada lifted the young girl from the fire, and thought that he had never seen before a maid so lovely. Her eyes were dark, and round her ivory forehead her black locks curled in profusion. Her shape was such that men's minds had never conceived its like. And King Drupada took the young girl to his palace and brought her up as his own daughter. Because of her curling black locks and beautiful deep eyes, King Drupada gave her the name of Krishna, or the dark maiden. But the subjects of King Drupada, because they thought that she was the King's daughter, always called the maid Draupadi. And as Draupadi she is known to this day.

The prowess shown by the sons of King Pandu, and above all Prince Arjuna's capture of King Drupada made the hatred of Prince Duryodhan burn still more hotly. Now King Dhritarashtra had named as his successor on the throne of the Bharatas, his nephew Prince Yudhishthira, because he was older than any of the King's own sons. And this, too, added fuel to the flames of Prince Duryodhan's hatred. He went to his blind father and filled his ears with lying tales about the pride of the Pandavas (for so men called the sons of King Pandu) and hinted falsely that they aspired to depose King Dhritarashtra and take from him the kingdom. The King believed his son, and repented bitterly that he had named as his heir his nephew, and not Prince Duryodhan. Seeing that the King's mind was turned against Prince Yudhishthira, the evil Prince Duryodhan unfolded to him a plan.

'Let the King,' said the cruel Prince, 'build a lovely palace of lac, at Varanavata. Let it be filled with only wooden furniture, and let the furniture and walls be soaked in oil, so that they may readily burn. Let the King induce by some means or other the five Pandavas and their mother to visit Varanavata and live in the palace. Then, if the King approves, I shall see to it that the palace takes fire, and that my cousins and Queen Kunti perish in the flames.'

King Dhritarashtra, in a weak and wicked moment, consented. And Prince Duryodhan got workmen to build at Varanavata a wooden palace all of lac, and filled it full of wooden articles all soaked in oil. When the palace was ready, Prince Duryodhan returned to Hastinapura. There he praised Varanavata and its beautiful palace, and told in such glowing words of the festival held there in honour of Shiva, the god of gods, that a desire to go thither seized Queen Kunti and her sons. 'Give us leave, O King,' they cried, 'to go to Varanavata and see its palace and Shiva's festival. For we shall have no peace until our eyes have rested on Varanavata and its wonders.' The King joyfully answered, 'Assuredly, my sister, thou hast leave to go there with thy sons. And with thee I will send a guard such as befits thy royal rank.' The King then ordered Prince Duryodhan to summon a guard. But over it the evil Prince placed a wicked captain, Purochan by name. And to him Prince Duryodhan told his plan. And the wicked Purochan promised that, when the Pandavas and their mother slept, he would set on fire the lac palace and see to it that they perished in the flames.

But Prince Vidura came to guess the cruel plot of Prince Duryodhan. Now Prince Vidura was half-brother of King Pandu and of King Dhritarashtra. But his mother was a slave girl, so he could never reign over Hastinapura. Yet although he was lowly born, he was a just and wise Prince, and he let fall before Prince Yudhishthira words dark, yet full of meaning to him who could interpret them. And Prince Yudhishthira, who was thoughtful beyond his years, knew from Vidura's words that he and his brothers and his mother were in grave danger.

When the Pandavas and Queen Kunti reached the palace at Varanavata, they marvelled greatly at its beauties. But Prince Yudhishthira saw that though the furniture and the tapestries were costly and beautiful, yet they were all soaked in oil. And he saw that the palace and roof were built only of wood or such other material as would easily burn. He called to him his mother and his brothers, and repeated to them the dark words of Prince Vidura and said, 'I fear, my mother, that we are in grave danger and the King or Prince Duryodhan seeks to burn us alive. Else why should the furniture and tapestries be soaked in oil and the palace walls and roof be made only of wood?' When the Pandavas saw through the wicked plot, they would have rushed out of the lac palace and would have hastened with all speed back to Hastinapura. But when they looked out of the windows, they saw that flight was impossible. For at every door Purochan, the wicked captain, had placed his guards. And if the Princes had rushed out, the guard would have cut them down or would have forced them again to enter the palace and would then have set fire to it. So perforce they stayed within, hoping that a good chance would come to them, by which they might escape.

Now the wise and good Prince Vidura had ever kept his nephews the Pandavas in his mind from the time when they had left Hastinapura. And he thought that if they could dig from the floor of the lac palace an underground passage which led into the forest outside, they might yet free themselves from the toils of the evil Prince Duryodhan. So Prince Vidura sent to Varanavata a skilful miner. He eluded the guards outside and made his way safely into the lac palace. There he told the Pandavas from whom he had come, and with their leave he dug an underground passage, which led from the floor of the palace into the woods outside. By night he worked and by day he hid his work by covering the mouth of the passage with wooden planks, so that Purochan, the wicked captain, should not guess that the Pandavas were planning flight. Now Purochan, the wicked captain, was awaiting a moonless night in which to set fire to the palace. And by means of this delay the miner sent by the good and wise Prince Vidura finished the digging of the passage.

The very night that the miner ended his work, the Pandavas lifted the planks from off the mouth of the passage and, descending into it, they and Queen Kunti walked until they reached the other mouth, that opened into the forest. There Prince Bhima bade his mother and brothers wait while he returned to the palace and had his revenge on the wicked captain, Purochan. They agreed, and Prince Bhima crawled back to the guard-house in which Purochan lived. Unseen by any of the guard, Prince Bhima set fire to the guard-house, and in its flames the guard and Purochan, their wicked captain, perished. But as the guard-house burned, a violent wind arose and blew the flames towards the lac palace, and it also took fire.

Now it so happened that on that same night a low-caste woman and her five sons had come to the lac palace to beg food. The Pandavas gave them food, meat, and wine, and they ate and drank until they lay down in a drunken stupor. As they lay asleep, the palace took fire and, all unconscious, they perished in the flames. When next morning the people of Varanavata awoke and went outside the city, they saw the smoking ashes of the lac palace and found within the charred remains of the low-caste woman and her sons. Seeing them, they thought that they were those of Queen Kunti and the Pandavas. And the men of Varanavata sorrowed greatly, for they loved the noble Princes and their stately mother. The news spread to Hastinapura also that Queen Kunti and her sons had died in the burning palace, and there, too, the citizens grieved for them sorely. When the evil Prince Duryodhan heard the news he told it to King Dhritarashtra, and they both thought that their cruel plot had succeeded. So they sorrowed not at all, but rejoiced exceedingly.

VII

HIDIMVA AND VAKA

AFTER Prince Bhima had set fire to the guard-house, he and his brothers and Queen Kunti fled southward through the forests until they came to the shores of the Ganges, queen of rivers. There they found a boat and a boatman, sent by the wise and good Prince Vidura so that they might cross the river and flee from the kingdom. When the boatman had ferried them across, the Pandavas and their mother disguised themselves as wandering Brahmans, and in this garb they fled farther and farther into the forests that grew on the southern shore of the great river. The farther they went, the steeper and the more rugged did the paths become and the undergrowth thicker and harder to cut through. At last Queen Kunti's strength wore out, so that Prince Bhima had to bear her on his back. When darkness fell, he placed her under the boughs of a banyan-tree, and made for her, as best he could, a bed of leaves. 'My son,' murmured the Queen faintly, 'I am very thirsty. Bring me water, or I die.'

So Prince Bhima went in search of water. North and south and east and west he searched, but in vain. At last there fell on his ears the cries of water-fowl, and then he knew that somewhere close by must be a lake. Forcing his way through the thick creepers, which grew between him and the spot from which the cries came, Prince Bhima at last found himself on the shore of a beautiful pool in the very heart of the forest. Tearing off his travel-stained clothes, he plunged into its sparkling depths and drank greedily. Then, filling a jar with water, he swiftly made his way back to the banyan-tree where he had left his mother.

Now after Prince Bhima had gone to fetch water, kindly sleep came to Queen Kunti and made her forget her thirst. And by her side, too, her four other sons stretched themselves in slumber. So when Prince Bhima returned with his jar full of water, he found his brothers and Queen Kunti fast asleep. He sat by their side and watched, so that no evil man or beast should come nigh to them or do them harm. And it was well that he did so. For close by there lived a man-eating monster, called Hidimva. He woke hungry before the eastern sky began to pale, and the morning breeze bore to him the scent of the weary mortals, who rested beneath the banyan-tree. Hidimva woke his sister, Hidimvi, who slept close to him, and bade her go forth and search for the rash men who had ventured into his kingdom, so that when she had found them, she might guide him to the spot and he might slay them.

Hidimvi went forth at her brother's bidding, and soon she spied the group who slept beneath the banyan-tree. Then close by she saw sitting, as a guard over them, the tireless Bhima. Her eyes rested first on his noble face and then on his deep chest and column-like arms, and she thought that in all her life she had never seen any one look as handsome as he did. And her love for her brother turned to hatred because he wished to slay and devour him whom now she longed to make her husband. Changing her monstrous form to that of a lovely girl, she drew near to Bhima. When he looked up at her, her face grew rosy with blushes, and her eyes fell before his. With faltering accents she said, 'Fair stranger, who art thou? and who are the men and the stately lady who sleep near thee? Thou, at least, must be one of the Immortals, who dwell in the heavens. For never before have I seen a face so noble as thine or a form so graceful.' Then she sighed as she added, 'But whoever thou art, flee from here, I pray thee, without a moment's delay. For thou and those with thee have strayed into the kingdom of my cruel brother Hidimva, and he soon will come here to slay and devour you. But when thou art gone, do not forget the maid who warned thee. For when my brother finds that you all are fled he will surely kill me.' Then Prince Bhima rose with a laugh and said, 'Fear not, fair maid. For I fear no man, nay, nor any monster upon the earth. If thy brother comes to slay and devour us, he will miss his dinner.'

As Prince Bhima spoke, the man-eating monster Hidimva rushed towards him, roaring. He had come to see why his sister did not return. And when he beheld her in human form and heard her exchanging kindly words with one of those whom he sought to devour, hot anger blazed up within him like a forest fire. 'Out upon thee,' he cried, 'false sister! I sent thee that thou mightest guide me to the slaying of these men, and now thou biddest them flee away! Traitress that thou art, I shall surely kill thee, after I have torn to pieces these friends of thine and devoured them.' As he spoke, he rushed with a snarl like that of a wild beast at Prince Bhima, and Prince Bhima rushed forward to meet him. Locked in each other's arms, they wrestled and fought up and down the open space in front of the banyan-tree, until the noise of their fighting awoke the Pandavas and the Queen. Prince Arjuna rose and, going close to the wrestlers said in mocking tones to Prince Bhima, 'Methinks, my brother, thou art weary with thy vigil. Else thou wouldst long ere this have slain this man-eater.' Stung by the taunt, Prince Bhima put forth all his strength and, lifting the monster high above him, dashed his head against the ground, so that he died instantly.

Hidimvi, the monster's sister, then came close to Prince Bhima and, looking fondly at him, said, 'Although thou hast slain my brother, I yet love thee more than all the world. Take me, I pray thee, for thy wife.' Prince Bhima looked at his mother, and Queen Kunti said, 'She loves thee, my son, and she risked her life to save thine. Go with her. I and thy brothers will go southwards until we find a town. There we will await thy coming.' So Prince Bhima left his brothers and Queen Kunti, and wandered through the pleasant woods with Hidimvi in a fair girl's shape. She showed him her brother's palace in the forest glade and the lakes which stretched close by, dotted with myriads of water-fowl. Many a happy day the Prince and Hidimvi passed together. But at last there arose in Prince Bhima's heart a longing to see again his brothers and Queen Kunti his mother. When Hidimvi learned his wish, she said sadly, 'I love thee, O Prince, so much that I cannot bear to keep thee against thy will. There is the path along which thy brothers and the Queen went. Follow it and thou wilt come to the town where they await thee. Fare thee well, but sometimes think kindly of Hidimvi who loved thee.' With these words and with many tears she embraced the Prince. He bade her farewell, and she watched his tall and strong form go southwards through the woods, until the trees hid him from her weeping eyes. Then she turned sadly to her forest home, for she knew that they had parted for ever.

Now Queen Kunti and her sons, after leaving Prince Bhima, had gone due southwards until they came to a town called Ekachakra, where, still dressed as Brahman beggars, they asked for and were given a lodging in the house of a Brahman who lived there. By day the brothers begged flour, and in the evening Queen Kunti baked it for them with her own hands. One day, when the sons had gone out to beg and she sat alone in the house, she heard the Brahman and his family talking to each other, as if in great sorrow. 'I shall go,' said the Brahman, 'for I cannot keep my life in exchange for either thine, my wife, or that of any of our children.' 'Nay, my husband,' sobbed the Brahman's wife, 'I must go in thy stead. For if thou diest, who will give bread to our little ones?' 'My parents,' interposed their daughter, 'you gave me life. It is for me now to repay your gift. You stay at home, and I shall go with the cart of food.'

The Queen rose and entered the room where the Brahman and his wife and his daughter were. 'My host,' said the Queen, 'what is thy trouble?' 'Our trouble is very great,' replied the Brahman. 'The town Ekachakra, in which we live, has been conquered by a fierce and a cruel chief called Vaka. In other respects he rules us well and guards us from our enemies. But every week we have to send him as food a cartful of rice, two buffaloes, and a man or woman from one of the townspeople's houses. To each house the turn comes in due order. And if the house to which the turn has come fails to send him his weekly tribute, he enters the town with his guards and slays and devours every man and woman in the house which has left his tribute unpaid. To-day the turn has come to our house, and we are trying to decide who among us shall go as Vaka's blood-tax with the cart of food.' The Queen thought for a moment, and then said with a sigh, 'If my son Bhima were but here, he would soon rid your town of this pest. But he is far away, wandering through the woods with the maid Hidimvi.' As the words left her lips, a shadow fell across the floor and, looking up, she saw that her son Bhima stood in the doorway. With a joyful cry she rose and said, 'Thou art welcome, my son,' and she told him the grief of the Brahman and the cruel tax laid on the town by the fierce chief Vaka. 'Have no fear, my mother,' said Bhima; 'I shall gladly go with the rice cart and try a fall with this pest of Ekachakra.'

That evening the Brahman filled a cart with rice, and, yoking to it two buffaloes, he made it over to Bhima. The Prince took the cart and drove it to a spot in the woods near which, as he had learned, the fierce chief, Vaka, had his dwelling. There Bhima called Vaka by name and sat down quietly and began to eat the rice from the cart. When Vaka heard his name called, he left his dwelling and came to where Bhima sat eating. Enraged at the sight, Vaka tore down the bough of a tree, and rushing at Bhima, aimed with it a fearful blow at the Prince's head. Bhima skilfully caught the branch in his left hand, and with his right gripped Vaka round the waist. Vaka, with the force of his own blow, fell forwards with Bhima above him. Bhima placed his knee on Vaka's back and said to him, 'It is time that the forest was rid of a pest like thee.' Then, seizing Vaka's neck with one hand and his waist-cloth with the other and pressing downwards with his knee, Bhima broke in two the backbone of the cruel chief. After he had died, Bhima dragged his body to one of the gates of the town, so that all the citizens of Ekachakra might know that they need pay the blood-tax no more to their wicked lord. When next morning the citizens saw his dead body lying by the gate, they clapped their hands, shouting and dancing with joy, and prostrated themselves in hundreds at Bhima's feet, because he had freed them from the monster Vaka.

After a few days had passed, Queen Kunti felt that she and her sons had stayed long enough as the guests of the Brahman of Ekachakra. So they thanked him for his kindness and set forth again on their wanderings. Now it so happened that about this time King Drupada of the Panchalas issued a proclamation. In it he invited all the Aryan Princes to come to Panchala and meet each other in an archery contest of which the prize was the hand of Draupadi the dark Princess, who had come to him in the sacrificial fire. For King Drupada knew that the Bharatas were all skilled men-at-arms, and he hoped that one or other of them would come to Panchala and there win the contest. In this way his curse would be fulfilled. For the Princess would enter the palace of the Bharatas and so would surely bring about their destruction as the voice from heaven had foretold.

It chanced that Queen Kunti and her sons came to one of the roads that led to Panchala city, and they saw that a great concourse of people was walking towards it. Seeing a company of Brahmans, Prince Yudhishthira asked their leader, 'Pray tell me, holy sir, why do men in such crowds go to Panchala city?' The Brahman looked at the

Prince and said, 'Methinks, sir, thou art a stranger in these parts. Or else thou wouldst surely know that King Drupada is to hold an archery contest and that he has promised to bestow on the winner the hand of his lovely daughter, the Princess Draupadi.'

When Prince Arjuna heard these words his eyes glittered, for he knew that in all India there was no archer his equal. So he whispered a word to his brother, and Yudhishthira turned again to the Brahman and said: 'Thou art right, holy sir, we are indeed strangers, and have heard nothing of this archery contest. But if thou and thy friends will give us leave, for we also are of the Brahman caste although very poor, we will gladly go in your company to Panchala. For we would fain see the archery contest and the lovely daughter of the King, the Princess Draupadi.' The Brahmans welcomed the Pandavas as fellow-travellers, and, marching by day and camping by night, they gradually drew near to Panchala city. At last they saw in front of them frowning walls and turreted gates, crowned with guards and archers. And one of the Brahmans said to the Pandavas, 'Fair sirs, we have come to our journey's end. The gates in front of us are those of King Drupada's city.'

VIII

THE WINNING OF DRAUPADI

WHEN the Pandavas and Queen Kunti entered the gates of Panchala, they parted with their friends the Brahman wayfarers, and as wandering Brahmans begged for themselves a lodging in a potter's house. Their food they begged from the crowds who had come to Panchala to see the Princes of India strive against each other for the hand of the lovely Draupadi.

Now King Drupada had prepared a mighty arena to the north-east of Panchala city. Round it he had built tiers and tiers of seats. Above them he had caused a canopy to be spread to shield the spectators from the sun's rays. The stairs that led to the seats were covered with rich carpets. Flowers hung down in festoons joining together the columns that supported the canopy.

On the day fixed for the judging, vast though the arena was, it was yet too small for the huge crowds of sightseers who sought to enter it, so that the guards at the doors had to turn them away in hundreds. At the appointed hour a Brahman priest entered the arena, and, after sacrificing to the Immortal Gods, he called down a blessing on the wooing of the Princes and prayed that the Immortals should order it that the bravest and most skilful suitor present should win the hand of King Drupada's daughter. When the prayers had ended, a door at the far end of the arena was flung wide open and every eye turned in that direction. Nor could any eye that had turned thither turn anywhere else, for it rested on a vision of beauty such as had never before been seen in all the lands of the Aryans. Surrounded by her serving women, clad in her robes of state, and sparkling with jewels, there entered with slow steps the lovely Princess, the dark maiden whom King Drupada had taken from the sacrificial fire. She was in the earliest spring of womanhood. And she bore in her hands the garland of flowers with which she was to deck the Prince whom the judges should proclaim the winner among her wooers. The heart of every suitor who gazed on her beat well-nigh to bursting. And each prayed to the god who had watched over his fathers to bestow on him tenfold strength and skill, that he might bear away the lovely Princess, the prize of the contest.

After the dark maiden had taken her seat high above the other spectators, the King's son, Prince Dhrishtadyumna rose from his throne, which was next to that of the Princess Draupadi, and spoke in a voice so clear and loud that it rang through the arena like the notes of a bugle call, saying, 'Hear, O ye Princes! He among you who possesses birth and beauty and strength, and would win for his wife this my sister Krishna, must shoot, from the bow which I shall give him, an arrow through a ring fastened high above the ground. Nor shall he be permitted to look directly at the mark. He must aim by gazing at the reflection of the ring in a tank of water at his feet.' He then sat down; and the Princes came forward to compete for the hand of the lovely Draupadi. To one after another of them Dhrishtadyumna gave the bow. But so stiff was its wood that one Prince after another tried in vain to bend it and had to leave the arena weeping with vexation, amid the laughter of the spectators.

Then a youth, tall and strong, whose name was Karna, stepped forward and, taking the bow lightly in his left hand, with his right pulled the string towards him until the points of the great bow began to draw near to each other. Now Karna was the son of the sun-god and Queen Kunti. For the sun-god had loved Queen Kunti when she was still a maiden, and to keep his birth secret she had hidden her newly-born son in a basket and had put it to float upon the Aswa river. The Aswa river bore the basket to the Ganges. And from the waves of the Ganges the kindly wife of a charioteer named Adhiratha had rescued the child and had adopted it as her own. None save the charioteer and his wife and Queen Kunti knew Karna's real birth, and all thought that he was but the son of Adhiratha. So when the Princess

Draupadi saw Karna take and bend the bow, her heart filled with scorn at the thought that a charioteer's son should seek her as his bride. She rose in her seat, and in a voice so sweet and high that her words sounded like the notes of a bell through the mighty arena, she cried, 'I shall never take as my husband the son of a charioteer!' When Karna heard her words, he threw down the bow and left the arena, hiding his vexation beneath feigned laughter, for his heart was raging with unquenchable anger.

Prince Dhrishtadyumna was about to dismiss the suitors and to announce that none was qualified to win his sister's hand when Prince Arjuna, in the guise of a Brahman beggar, strode into the arena. At first the other suitors laughed to see a Brahman beggar hope to win where they, the heirs of great kingdoms, had failed. But when they saw Prince Arjuna's mighty arms, deep chest, and noble bearing, they held their peace and watched him with bated breath and anxious eyes. Prince Arjuna took the bow, twanged the bowstring, and drew it towards him without seeming effort. Then gazing steadfastly at the reflection of the ring in the tank of water close to his feet, he drew the bowstring to his ear and let the arrow fly.

So surely aimed was the shaft that it rose right through the very centre of the ring. And the myriad spectators cheered and shouted with joy and showered garlands on the gallant young wooer, who had done the task set him. But the Princes who had failed to bend the bow gathered in a dark mass at the far end of the arena. And one muttered to the other, 'Who is this Brahman beggar who dares to woo a royal Princess? How can a Kshatriya maiden wed one of another caste? Let us kill this vagabond and carry off the lovely Draupadi and draw lots for her among ourselves!'

And they rushed at Prince Arjuna and would have torn him limb from limb, had his brothers not hastened to his help. To Prince Arjuna's right side went his brother the wise Yudhishthira. To his left side went the giant Bhima. And to the sides of Yudhishthira and Bhima stepped those two matchless swordsmen Nakula and Sahadev. When the Princes saw the mighty frames and resolute faces of the five Brahman beggars, they drew back again towards the far end of the arena. For their hearts sank within them.

But Karna, from whom rage, because of the slight put upon him, had cast out fear, strode forward and challenged Prince Arjuna to fight. And Prince Shalya, who had come from Madra, a far land, in the hope of winning Draupadi, challenged Prince Bhima to wrestle with him. But Prince Arjuna gave Karna such a buffet that he rolled senseless on the ground. And Prince Bhima lifted Shalya in his arms, as if he had been a child, and threw him clear over the arena walls, but with such dexterity that Shalya landed on his feet and felt no hurt. When the other Princes saw what had befallen Karna and Shalya, they slunk crestfallen out of the arena and went to their various homes. Then Prince Arjuna walked to the foot of the throne, from which the lovely Princess Draupadi was gazing at him in fond admiration. With a loving smile she placed her garland round Prince Arjuna's neck. Then he knew that he had won her heart until death should part them. And through the cheering crowds he led Draupadi with him out of the arena.

Now Queen Kunti had not gone to the archery contest, but had stayed behind at the potter's hut. As time passed and the Pandavas did not return, she began to revolve in her mind the possible dangers which might have befallen them. At last she heard Arjuna's footstep without. And she heard him say, 'Lo! mother, we have to-day secured abundant alms!' The Queen, not knowing that he spoke in jest and meant by 'alms' the lovely Princess Draupadi, replied joyfully, 'It is well, my sons; share the alms all five of you.' When she had spoken and Prince Arjuna led before her the dark maid of the Panchalas Queen Kunti realized too late that she had ordered the lovely Princess to be the bride of all her five sons.

When Prince Dhrishtadyumna bestowed on Prince Arjuna his blushing sister, he wondered greatly who the five Brahman beggars could be. Their noble bearing betrayed them to be no beggars, but sons of kings. The archery of one of them was such that only Prince Arjuna could have equalled it. The strength of him who had hurled Shalya out of the arena must be no less than that of Prince Bhima. The beggars, moreover, numbered five, just as the Pandavas did. But then all men thought that the Pandavas had perished in the flames of the Varanavata palace. Prince Dhrishtadyumna resolved to spy on them and find out who these seeming beggars were. He traced them to the potter's cottage and hid himself close by. In no long time he heard Queen Kunti's voice. She was instructing the Princess Draupadi how to serve with food Prince Arjuna and his brothers. 'First,' said Queen Kunti, 'give half of all the food cooked to Prince Bhima. For his giant frame needs as much as do all the others. Then divide the remaining half between Yudhishthira, Arjuna, Nakula, Sahadev, myself, and yourself.'

When Prince Dhrishtadyumna heard the Queen utter their names, he crept out of his hiding-place and made his way back to King Drupada's palace. There he told the King, his father, that the five Brahman beggars were the Pandavas disguised, and that he who had won the dark Princess was none other than Prince Arjuna, the greatest bowman in all the lands of the Aryans. When King Drupada heard the news brought him by his son, he rejoiced mightily, for he knew well the hatred which Prince Duryodhan bore to his cousins. And he guessed that through this hatred his curse would bear good fruit and bring about the destruction of the Bharatas. He sent a priest to call the Brahman beggars to his palace. There they owned, in answer to King Drupada's questions, that they were the sons of King Pandu, who had ruled over the wide lands of Hastinapura.

King Drupada loudly expressed his joy that he who had won the hand of the dark Princess was Prince Arjuna, and therefore of gentle blood. And he said that he would without delay make ready for the nuptials of the Prince and his daughter. Then Yudhishthira arose from his seat and said, 'O King, the Princess Draupadi must wed all five of us in turn, and not only my younger brother Arjuna.' And he told the King how the Queen had said, 'My sons, share the alms all five of you,' and he added that however strange such a marriage might seem, it was better that it should take place than that the word of an Aryan Queen should be set aside. But King Drupada was loath to consent. So he referred the matter to a very holy seer called Vyasa. And Vyasa, after hearing both King Drupada and Prince Yudhishthira, ruled that, strange though such a marriage might be, it was yet sinless. And it was better that it should take place than that the saying of an Aryan Queen should go unheeded. King Drupada perforce gave his consent, and, summoning his friends and kinsmen and nobles, he held a mighty feast in honour of the wedding. On an auspicious day he gave the Princess Draupadi in marriage to the Prince Yudhishthira. And on four successive days he gave her in turn to Prince Bhima, Prince Arjuna, Prince Nakula, and Prince Sahadev. Thus it came about that the five Pandavas wedded and took to their home the lovely dark maiden, the Princess Draupadi, who rose from the sacrificial fire to bring about the ruin of the Bharatas.

IX

THE ADVENTURES OF PRINCE ARJUNA

THE spies of Prince Duryodhan soon brought to him the unwelcome news that the Pandavas had not perished in the Varanavata palace, but had escaped, and that, in the guise of Brahman beggars, they had won the hand of the lovely Princess Draupadi, the daughter of the King of the Panchalas. When Prince Duryodhan heard what the spies told him he was sad at heart. For he feared that with the army of the Panchalas the Pandavas would attack the Elephant City and that, such was their prowess, the Panchala army led by them might drive King Dhritarashtra from the throne of the Bharatas. So Prince Duryodhan and King Dhritarashtra took counsel together, and they talked over the various ways by which they might cause dissension among the Pandavas, so that they might fight with and slay each other, and so free King Dhritarashtra and Prince Duryodhan from the fear of their vengeance.

But among King Dhritarashtra's counsellors was the wise old Prince Bhishma, his uncle. His mother was the mighty Ganges river. And she had borne him fourscore years before to King Shantanu, the father of King Vichitravirya. Indeed, he would have succeeded to the throne of the Bharatas, had he not willingly resigned the throne to his younger brother. And Prince Bhishma rebuked his nephew for trying to slay the Pandavas. He bade the King Dhritarashtra call the Pandavas back again and give them half his kingdom as the share of King Pandu. King Dhritarashtra hearkened to his wise old counsellor's word, and he sent his brother Prince Vidura to Panchala with splendid presents and a pressing message that they should return to Hastinapura. When Prince Yudhishthira and his brothers saw Prince Vidura come to Panchala, they welcomed him gladly, and they joyously agreed to return to Hastinapura and forgive the past. When they reached Hastinapura, King Dhritarashtra greeted them kindly, and in Prince Bhishma's presence bestowed on them half his kingdom. Then, taking leave of the King, they went with Draupadi to the lands allotted them. And there they built a city so fair that men called it Indraprastha, for, so they said, the god Indra would not have scorned to live in it. And its ruins may still be seen near Delhi and are called Indrapad to this day.

While the Princes lived with the Princess Draupadi at Indraprastha, there came to them a Brahman suppliant who begged for justice. And, as Prince Yudhishthira was in the inner room of the Princess Draupadi, the Brahman suppliant sought out Prince Arjuna. To him the Brahman related how thieves had set upon him in the realm of Indraprastha and taken away his wealth. And he called aloud for justice and prayed Prince Arjuna to go forth and slay the robbers and restore to him his wealth. When Prince Arjuna heard the suppliant's prayers, he went, unbidden by Prince Yudhishthira, into the Princess Draupadi's inner room, and there Prince Yudhishthira gave him leave to avenge the wrongs done to the Brahman suppliant. So Prince Arjuna donned his armour and sprang into his chariot. He soon overtook the thieves as they were fleeing with the Brahman's wealth. He shot them all down with his arrows and, placing their spoil on his chariot, he drove back to Indraprastha and gave it back to the Brahman, who went homewards rejoicing greatly.

Now when the Pandavas had taken the Princess Draupadi to wife, they had bound themselves by an oath that, if one of them entered unbidden the rooms of the Princess Draupadi when another Pandava was already there, he who so entered unbidden should exile himself into the forest. And so it came to pass that Prince Arjuna had to exile himself into the forest, or break his oath. But he was young and strong and brave. So, taking his bow and arrows and his armour, he sprang lightly into his chariot, and was gone like a flash of lightning out of Indraprastha and towards the southern forests.

For many days he wandered free from care, living on the game which he shot by his bow and arrows. Then in due time he came to the Ganges river. And its water looked so clear and bright that Prince Arjuna flung aside his garments and plunged into the stream. While he swam in midstream, a water-nymph named Ulupi fell in love with him and dragged him beneath the surface to her palace far below the Ganges river. And Prince Arjuna looked on Ulupi and thought her very fair. Yet he would not stay with her or be her husband as she wished, but bade her good-bye. And as she embraced him sadly she said to him, 'Although thou wilt not stay with me, I yet will give thee this as my parting present, that thou shalt never be conquered by any creature that lives in the waters.'

Then, leaving the Ganges, Prince Arjuna wandered on until he came to the sea-shore. And at a spot where a river flowed into the sea, a band of holy men had made their dwelling-place. When

Prince Arjuna saw them, he begged for their blessing. And when they had blessed him, he told them that he wished to bathe in the waters of the river. But they tried to dissuade him. 'The river,' they said, 'is haunted by a man-eating alligator. And, if thou bathest, it will surely devour thee as it has devoured others.'

But Prince Arjuna, in the pride of his youth and courage, laughed at their warning, and, stripping off his garments, he plunged into the cool waters of the river. He had hardly swum into midstream when he felt an alligator's jaws seize him by the leg. And, strive as he might, he could not free himself. His strength was ebbing fast from pain and from his efforts to swim to shore, and he had all but given himself up to death. Suddenly the words of the nymph Ulupi flashed across his brain.—'Although thou wilt not stay with me, I yet will give thee this as my parting present, that thou shalt never be conquered by any creature that lives in the waters.' Then his courage revived and with all his remaining strength he swam for the shore, dragging the alligator after him. When he reached a spot where he could stand he drove his thumbs into the alligator's eyes until the monster loosed his hold. Then, seizing it round the body with his arms, he flung it ashore as if it had been a log that had floated down with the current. And lo! directly the alligator fell on the dry ground it changed its shape and became a lovely girl, who smiled at Prince Arjuna from the bank.

Prince Arjuna could scarcely gather voice to ask the maid the cause of what had happened. But she replied, with a laugh that made her look even fairer than before:

'Prince Arjuna, I once was a water-nymph and beautiful as thou seest me now. And there were four other nymphs, my friends, who were as fair as

I, and wherever I went they never failed to go also. One day we came to the hermitage of a holy man who had given up the world and its beauties and its temptations and lived all by himself, worshipping the gods in a lonely forest glade. When we saw him we thought we would make him break his vows. And we smiled at him and embraced him and tried in a hundred ways to make his thoughts turn from the gods to us. But we tried in vain. After warning us several times, he at last lost all patience. Praying to the gods, he called down on us a terrible curse. And the curse was that we should become alligators and remain so for a hundred years. We threw ourselves at his feet and begged him to forgive us. But he would not wholly take back his curse, and he said, "O nymphs! I have cursed you, and alligators you will become. But you may regain your forms once more when a hero, by name Arjuna the Pandava, comes and drags you to land."

'And thus, as thou didst overcome me, O Prince, and didst drag me to shore, I know that thou art Prince Arjuna the Pandava. And I have yet another boon to ask of thee, which is to come with me where my sister nymphs dwell in various spots as alligators, so that thou mayst drag them ashore also and they may regain their forms as water-nymphs.'

Prince Arjuna readily agreed and, going with the water-nymph to the various spots where her sister nymphs had as alligators hidden themselves, he plunged boldly into the waters and dragged them one after another ashore. One after another they became beautiful smiling girls. And when all five had regained their former shapes, they embraced Prince Arjuna and thanked him each in turn. And then, with smiles on their rosy lips, they dived beneath the water of the river near them, and Prince Arjuna's eyes never rested on them again.

On the same night when the water-nymphs had bidden Prince Arjuna farewell, there came to the Prince a vision. In it he saw a Brahman sage with matted locks and ragged garments, who approached him. But as the sage came closer Prince Arjuna saw that, ragged and unkempt though he was, his eyes blazed like the rising sun and his skin shone as if lit up by some divine light within. And Prince Arjuna thought to himself, 'This must be one of the Immortals who rule the broad heavens.'

But the Brahman came ever closer and said, 'O Pandava, I am the fire-god Agni, and I desire thy help to burn the Khandava forest. In it there dwells an evil race called the Nagas or serpent-men. For they are the offspring of the poisonous snakes, who dwell underground, and of the women whom the serpents have taken captive. And they are a wicked race who prey upon the Aryans that live near the Ganges, and I would gladly burn these Nagas to death with the forest in which they dwell. But, although I try ever so much to consume the Khandava forest, I can never do so. For the god Indra, whom the Nagas worship, loves and protects them. And whenever I strive to devour the forest with my flames, the god Indra pours down rain upon it. And the rain quenches my flames, and the evil race of the Nagas live on and continue to do evil and all kinds of cruelty and wickedness. Therefore, O Pandava Prince, I crave thy help. For, so men say, thou art the son of the god Indra, and thus thou shalt be able to guard me against thy father. But because thou art a mortal man, and hast only mortal weapons, I have brought thee the Gandiva bow and its inexhaustible quiver, which I have begged for thee from Varuna, the sea-god.

And with it in thy hands, we two shall surely destroy utterly the evil race of the Nagas.'

When Prince Arjuna awoke with a start, the Brahman had vanished. But close by his side Prince Arjuna saw a mighty bow and a quiver full of arrows. Then he knew that the fire-god Agni had really visited him as he slept. Prince Arjuna rose and, taking the bow, set out to the Khandava forest. When he reached its borders he cried out in a loud voice, 'Now, O Fire King, I am ready.' And as the words left his lips, the whole forest in front of him caught fire and blazed with a mighty roar. A strong wind, too, arose, and Prince Arjuna thought that in a few minutes the whole forest would be consumed. But, just as the thought came into his mind, he heard a mighty clap of thunder. Looking upwards he saw that great masses of clouds were hastening together from all quarters of the sky, and in a few more moments there arose a mighty storm. Rain poured down from heaven and fell upon the fire, and, as the rain fell, the flames grew gradually weaker and weaker. And Prince Arjuna knew that the god Indra had come to help the Nagas.

X

ARJUNA AND SUBHADRA

WHEN Prince Arjuna saw the flames dying down, he knew that the time had come for him to act. He drew the arrows out of the quiver which he had found by his side when he woke from his sleep, and shot them as fast as he could into the air. And directly he took one arrow out of the quiver, another took its place. For the quiver of the sea-god Varuna was inexhaustible. When Prince Arjuna shot the arrows, they rose so far into the sky that it was long before they fell to earth. And in this way the arrows rising and falling formed a roof above the Khandava forest, so that the god Indra's rain poured down on each side of it and hardly a drop fell among the trees. And the flames, sheltered from the rain, burst forth with renewed strength until they had gripped firmly the entire forest. The Nagas, seeing that the god Indra could no longer save them, rushed out of every corner of the woods. But fast as they fled, the arrows drawn by Prince Arjuna from his inexhaustible quiver flew faster still. One by one, he slew the entire race of the Nagas save only one, by name Moya. He rushed to Prince Arjuna's feet and prayed for mercy. No Aryan warrior would kill a suppliant foe. So Prince Arjuna gave Moya his life, but made him his slave. And he bade Moya go to Indraprastha and there serve the Pandavas.

After the burning of the Khandava forest, Prince Arjuna made his way to the lands of King Krishna of Dwarka. As Arjuna strayed among the Dwarka Hills, he saw a maiden fairer than any in all the world, save only the dark maiden of Panchala. In spite of her cries and tears and the resistance of her serving-men, the Prince caught her up in his arms and bore her off in his chariot. As the days of his exile were over, Arjuna turned his horses' heads towards Indraprastha. As he drove, he thought to himself: 'The last maiden whom I won I shared with my brothers, but this maiden I shall keep as my own.'

Now the maid whom he had borne away was Subhadra, the sister of King Krishna.[1] When the news came to Dwarka that a stranger had carried off the Princess of the city, King Krishna and his brother Balarama called out all their horsemen and rode furiously after the stranger that they might

1 See Appendix A.

win her back. But as they followed the path of the fugitives they came to know that the captor of Subhadra was Prince Arjuna the Bharata. King Krishna then bethought him that if the Prince married his sister no harm would be done. For high though her rank was, it was not higher than that of a scion of the great house of Hastinapura. So he sent his swiftest horseman after the Prince. And the messenger overtook Arjuna and bade him come back in peace and wed the maid. So Arjuna returned with the horseman to Dwarka, and King Krishna prepared a mighty feast, and to it he called all the nobles of his kingdom. And in the presence of the great gathering, King Krishna gave the lovely Princess Subhadra to Prince Arjuna to be his own bride and not to be shared by him with his brothers.

Gladly the maid took the hero as her husband. Joyously they drove together to Indraprastha. Joyously, too, the wise Prince Yudhishthira and his brothers welcomed back the brave Arjuna. And they shouted until the rafters echoed, as they listened to the story of his doings in the southern forests. Then Prince Arjuna took Subhadra by the hand and led her to the room of the Princess Draupadi. But here no joyous greeting awaited him. For the dark Princess of the Panchalas loved Prince Arjuna best of all her lords, and her heart was sore within her because he had won for himself another bride. But Subhadra threw herself at Draupadi's feet and vowed that she would ever serve the dark Princess as a waiting maid. At length the Princess Draupadi forgave Prince Arjuna. And once again the Pandavas were all united in love with each other and with the dark maiden of the Panchalas.

Not long after Prince Arjuna's return to Indraprastha, Moya, the captive Naga whose life Prince

Arjuna had spared, came before the wise Prince Yudhishthira. 'O Prince,' said the Naga Moya, 'I wish to build thee a palace worthy of the great house to which thou dost belong.' Now the Nagas were skilled above all men in building cities and palaces. And among all the Nagas there was no artificer so skilful as Moya. So when Prince Yudhishthira heard the words of Moya, he rejoiced greatly and bade the Naga Moya begin the palace without delay. The captive Naga waited until an auspicious day came. He then measured out a piece of land 5,000 cubits square for the foundations. Thereon he built a palace so lofty and spacious that no Aryan Prince had ever seen its like. And he revealed to Prince Yudhishthira the places where the Naga nobles and merchants had hidden their treasure and jewels, before they fled from the Khandava forest to their death. And with the treasures and jewels of the Naga nobles and merchants Prince Yudhishthira adorned the palace in a way so splendid that no palace has ever been so adorned either before or since.

With the rest of the Naga treasure Prince Yudhishthira fitted out armies and placed over them his four brothers and sent them in all directions, so that they might levy tribute from the Kings of India. Prince Arjuna levied tribute from all the Aryan Kings who dwelt north of the Ganges. The mighty Prince Bhima led an army into Bengal and returned with vast spoils torn from the wealthy chiefs who lived where Ganges, Queen of rivers, rushes to join herself to Ocean. Prince Nakula subdued the wild tribes who dwelt along the Indus, and Prince Sahadev forced the barbarians of Southern India to pay taxes to Prince Yudhishthira as their overlord.

When his brothers had returned to Indraprastha laden with the wealth taken from all the four quarters of India, Prince Yudhishthira thought that, like the great King Harischandra of olden days, he would hold a Rajasuya sacrifice. Now he who held a Rajasuya sacrifice thereby proclaimed that he was the greatest ruler in all India, and at the sacrifice all the other Kings and Princes had to do him service. And Prince Yudhishthira believed that, because of his brothers' victories, he had in truth become the greatest ruler in all India. But before he ordered the sacrifice to be made ready, he sent for King Krishna of Dwarka, whose sister Subhadra Prince Arjuna had borne away and wedded. King Krishna came in answer to Prince Yudhishthira's message. And when the King had come to him, Prince Yudhishthira asked his advice; for King Krishna was wise and experienced above all other Indian Kings. When Prince Yudhishthira had ended his speech, King Krishna answered: 'O Prince, until thou hast killed Jarasandha, King of Magadha, thou shouldst not perform the Rajasuya sacrifice. For he is the strongest of the Aryan Kings, and until thou hast slain him thou hast no right to boast that thou art the greatest ruler in all India nor to hold the Rajasuya sacrifice.'

Prince Yudhishthira asked many questions about Jarasandha, King of Magadha, and King Krishna told him that Jarasandha was a wicked and cruel King, who had vowed that he would take captive and sacrifice to the great god Shiva an hundred other Kings. He had already seized and thrown into his dungeons eighty-six Kings. And when he had seized fourteen more, he meant to torture to death his hundred captives as a sacrifice to Shiva, God of Gods, whom he worshipped. Prince Yudhishthira raged to think that anywhere among the lands of the Aryans there lived such a cruel King. And he vowed that he would straightway send an army to destroy his capital and bring King Jarasandha a captive to

Indraprastha. But King Krishna told Prince Yudhishthira that so mighty and well-armed were the hosts of Magadha that not even the Pandavas and their warriors could destroy it.

When Yudhishthira heard the King's reply, he was at a loss what to do. But the wise and experienced King Krishna gave him cunning advice. 'Do not despair, O Prince,' said King Krishna, 'for there is yet a way by which King Jarasandha can be slain. If Prince Bhima can enter his palace in disguise and challenge the King to a wrestling match, all will be well. For King Jarasandha is an Aryan King. And he cannot in honour refuse a challenge. He is, moreover, a strong and skilful wrestler. And he has overthrown and slain all those with whom he has hitherto wrestled. So he will not fear to try his strength even against the mighty Prince Bhima.'

When Prince Yudhishthira heard the cunning words of the wise and experienced King Krishna, he sent for his brothers Prince Bhima and Prince Arjuna. And it was agreed that King Krishna and the Prince Bhima and Arjuna should disguise themselves as Brahman beggars and so gain an entry into Magadha. Once there, they, as holy men, would ask an audience from the cruel King. When face to face with him, so that he could not in honour refuse, Prince Bhima would challenge him to a wrestling match. Everything turned out as King Krishna had planned. Without weapons of any kind and in rags that barely covered their nakedness, King Krishna and the Princes Bhima and Arjuna set out towards Magadha. When they came to the gates, the guards let them through, deeming them to be wandering beggars. When they reached the palace door, they, as Brahmans, prayed for an audience with King Jarasandha.

Now King Jarasandha, wicked and cruel though

he was, was loth to insult the holy caste by refusing these ragged Brahmans an audience. He bade his chamberlain lead them to his audience chamber. When they had come near to his throne, he offered them alms, but these they angrily rejected. Marvelling greatly, King Jarasandha asked them their business. King Krishna in reply said, 'O King Jarasandha, the cup of thine iniquities and thy cruelties has long been full. I bid thee release the Kings whom thou keepest captive in thy cruel dungeons or wrestle with this our leader,' and he pointed to Prince Bhima, 'to the death.'

King Jarasandha was an Aryan King, and as such he could not in honour refuse a challenge. Moreover, as a mighty warrior and wrestler, he looked with joy at the huge shoulders and thighs of Prince Bhima. And he rejoiced greatly to meet a wrestler with whom he might wrestle on equal terms. Scornfully he said, 'I refuse to let loose any of the captive Kings from my dungeons, and with thy leader yonder I will gladly wrestle to the death.'

With these words King Jarasandha flung aside his crown and his royal robes, and girt up his loins and made himself ready for the wrestling. Then he and Prince Bhima gripped each other after the manner of Aryan wrestlers. For many a long hour the two struggled and panted, locked in each other's deadly embrace. And in all the fights in which Prince Bhima took part, he never came so near to defeat as in this one. But at last King Jarasandha's strength began to fail. With one supreme effort Prince Bhima lifted the King off the ground, and whirling him round his head flung him face downwards on the floor. Then placing his knee on Jarasandha's back, Bhima broke it in two, so that the King died instantly.

After killing Jarasandha, King Krishna and the

two Pandava Princes fled swiftly out of Magadha. When they reached Indraprastha, Yudhishthira called together an army and placed Prince Bhima over it. With it he marched against Magadha and took it easily. For, bewildered at the death of King Jarasandha, the Magadha armies were in confusion and the generals at variance. Then Prince Bhima unlocked the cruel dungeons and set free the captive Kings, who threw themselves at the Prince's feet, thanking him for their deliverance. And, on returning to their homes, they sent in their gratitude rich presents to Indraprastha.

After spoiling Magadha and taking back with him all King Jarasandha's treasures, Prince Bhima returned in triumph. And on his return the wise and experienced King Krishna said to Prince Yudhishthira: 'Now, O Prince, thou canst celebrate the Rajasuya sacrifice.'

XI

YUDHISHTHIRA'S GAMBLING

WHEN Prince Yudhishthira heard the words of the wise and experienced King Krishna of Dwarka, he resolved to hold a Rajasuya sacrifice. To every quarter of India he sent his heralds, bidding all the Kings and Princes of India attend his court at Indraprastha, so that they might do him homage and acclaim him the overlord of all the East. And they dared not disobey the bidding, for they all knew that if they did, Prince Yudhishthira would send against them his brothers at the head of armies and would storm their cities and spoil them of their wealth. So all the Kings and Princes of India went in state to Indraprastha. And bringing with them gifts of every kind, they offered them with their homage to Prince Yudhishthira the Bharata.

But to King Dhritarashtra Prince Yudhishthira merely sent an invitation to come as spectator. For the King was Yudhishthira's uncle, and he would not slight him willingly. And Prince Yudhishthira bade all the other Kings and Princes do for him menial service. But he asked Prince Duryodhan only to take the jewels from the hand of those who brought them as gifts. The Kings and Princes, fearing to refuse, did menial service for Prince Yudhishthira. But when they had done his bidding, he gave to each of them presents of greater value than those which he had taken from them. And at the close of the sacrifice all the Kings and Princes present sprinkled holy water over Prince Yudhishthira, and then went home, bearing the Prince's costly presents, each to his own city.

But the heart of the evil Prince Duryodhan was tormented with envy at the sight of his cousin's splendour and greatness. And as he strayed through the wondrous palace which the Naga captive Moya had built, Prince Duryodhan fell into a tank of water in the centre of one of the halls. For with such cunning had Moya laid down and polished the crystal floor that he who walked on it could not tell where the crystal ended and the water began. When Duryodhan, with sullen face and dripping clothes, pulled himself out of the water-tank, Prince Bhima's mighty shoulders shook with laughter at his cousin's plight. And in bitter wrath and vowing vengeance, Duryodhan returned with King Dhritarashtra to Hastinapura. Now one of Prince Duryodhan's kinsmen was Shakuni, King of Gandhara, who was skilled above all men in gambling and especially in throwing the dice. To King Shakuni Duryodhan went and poured out the whole bitterness of his soul. 'Unless,' he said, 'I can revenge myself on Prince Yudhishthira, and his brothers, I shall take my own

KING SHAKUNI COMFORTS PRINCE DURYODHAN

life. For life is but a long torment, O King, to one so stung with jealousy and hatred as I am.'

Shakuni, King of Gandhara, thought for a moment. Then a cunning smile spread over his face as he replied: 'Nay, my kinsman Duryodhan, there is no need to take thy life. I have thought of a device, whereby we shall ruin Prince Yudhishthira and his brothers. Thou knowest, O Duryodhan, that Prince Yudhishthira is fond of gambling, but knows little of the art of throwing the dice. Whereas I, Shakuni, surpass all men in gambling and especially in the game of dice. Do thou, therefore, bid King Dhritarashtra call all the nobles of Hastinapura to his court to gamble, and bid him at the same time invite the Pandavas also. When they are come, I shall challenge Prince Yudhishthira to a game of dice. He is an Aryan Prince and his pride will not suffer him to refuse the challenge. When the play has begun, he will lose all his wisdom because of his love for the dice. And I shall win from him his wealth and his armies and his kingdom, and I shall give them to thee to do as thou wilt with them.'

When Duryodhan heard Shakuni's words he was wellnigh overcome with joy, and went as swiftly as he could to King Dhritarashtra's presence. To his father the evil Prince unfolded his plan. And the King, approving it, sent forth heralds to bid all the nobles of Hastinapura come and gamble in his assembly hall. The nobles gladly hearkened to the heralds and came, all of them, to the King's assembly hall. And to his nephews the Pandavas King Dhritarashtra sent the wise and good Prince Vidura. For the King knew that his nephews loved Vidura and would be loth to refuse an invitation conveyed by him. Vidura drove to Indraprastha, and with fitting words conveyed the King's message. Prince Yudhishthira with fitting words agreed to attend the King's assembly. And putting on their most splendid robes, the Pandavas and the Princess Draupadi drove in their chariots of state from Indraprastha to Hastinapura. At Hastinapura Prince Duryodhan welcomed them with treacherous smiles, and with every courtesy took them to the royal rooms reserved for them.

Next morning when the Pandavas presented themselves at the assembly hall, it was already thronged with the nobles of Hastinapura, all deeply engaged in gambling with each other. When Prince Yudhishthira had done obeisance to his uncle, the cunning Shakuni, King of Gandhara, rose from his seat and said, 'Welcome, my kinsman Yudhishthira: come with me, I pray thee, and let us gamble with the dice.' Prince Yudhishthira begged that King Shakuni would excuse him. 'I am but a poor dicer,' he said, 'and I am in no way a match for thee in skill, King Shakuni.' Then Shakuni said, with a mocking laugh, 'Methinks, fair kinsman, thou didst wrong to hold a Rajasuya sacrifice. Thou wouldst call thyself, forsooth, the greatest warrior in all India. And yet thou art afraid of a battle with me, even though the weapons be only dice.'

Now Prince Yudhishthira was an Aryan Prince. And when King Shakuni taunted him with feeling fear, the pride within him blazed up like a forest fire. And working through his pride, the curse called down from heaven by King Drupada robbed Prince Yudhishthira of all his caution and wisdom. 'Nay, King Shakuni,' he cried hotly, 'I am an Aryan Prince, and I fear no man upon this earth, and thee least of all. As thou hast challenged me to a dicing match, I accept thy challenge. Let the game begin forthwith.' Then the cunning King Shakuni smiled a sweet smile and said softly, 'Nay, my kinsman, be not wroth, I did not wish to anger thee.' And he and Prince Yudhishthira sat down to throw dice against each other. Against King Shakuni's matchless skill as a dicer, such little skill as Prince Yudhishthira had availed him nothing. He lost stake after stake. At last his brothers, pressing round him, bade him cease. But the curse called down on the Bharatas by King Drupada, working through Yudhishthira's pride, would not suffer him to own himself vanquished. Stake by stake, he gambled away his wealth and his elephants, his armies and his palace, his slaves and his kingdom.

At last, he had nothing left in all the world except his four brothers, himself, and the lovely dark Princess, whom Prince Arjuna had won in the archery contest at Panchala. Nevertheless Prince Yudhishthira would not yield. He staked in turn Prince Nakula, Prince Sahadev, Prince Arjuna, and Prince Bhima, and lost them. Then, mad with rage and despair, he staked himself and lost again. Then the cunning King Shakuni said, with a mocking laugh, 'Do not yet give up all hope of winning, my kinsman. Thou canst still stake Draupadi the dark Princess of the Panchalas.' Stung by King Shakuni's laugh, Prince Yudhishthira replied, 'King Shakuni, I stake Draupadi the lovely dark Princess whom my brother Arjuna won on the archery ground of the Panchalas.' The King and the Prince each threw the dice. The King looked at them. Then with a joyous laugh he said to Prince Yudhishthira, 'Fortune has treated thee ill to-day, my kinsman. As thou seest, thou hast lost thy last stake, Draupadi the dark Princess of the Panchalas.'

In this way Prince Yudhishthira and his brothers, because of the curse called down on the Bharatas by King Drupada, fell into the net spread for them by the evil Prince Duryodhan. When the dicing was ended, the Pandavas had lost their kingdom and their wealth and their elephants and their armies. And they and the dark Princess Draupadi became the slaves of Prince Duryodhan. For, as agreed beforehand, King Shakuni bestowed all his winnings on the Prince Duryodhan. Then the Prince in a loud, haughty voice said to his brother Dushasan, 'Bring me here my slave Draupadi. It is time that she took her place among my serving women.' So Prince Dushasan went to the Princess Draupadi's room and, telling her all that had happened, bade her go with him and take her place among Prince Duryodhan's serving women.

The Princess followed her cousin to the King's assembly hall. There she proudly faced Prince Duryodhan and all the nobles of Hastinapura, and in clear, ringing tones she said, 'O King Dhritarashtra, I pray for justice. When Prince Yudhishthira staked himself and lost, he became a slave. He, therefore, could own nothing himself. And as he could own nothing, he did not own me. Thus he could not stake me and lose me to King Shakuni. His stake, therefore, was void, and I am not the slave of Prince Duryodhan.' When she had spoken these words, the King answered nothing. So the dark Princess sought shelter amongst the ladies of Queen Gandhari, the wife of King Dhritarashtra.

But Prince Dushasan ran after the Princess in a fury and, seizing her by the hair, dragged her back into the middle of the assembly room. And into his mind, because of the curse of King Drupada, there came an evil thought. 'I shall humble thee, thou proud Princess,' he cried. 'I shall strip off thy robes and set thee naked before all the nobles of Hastinapura.' And, as he spoke, he seized Draupadi's garments and strove to tear them off her. But one of the kindly Immortals took pity on the sorrow of the dark Princess, and ordered it so that Prince Dushasan tore off her garments in vain. For as fast as he pulled them off, the god clothed her with fresh ones. At last Dushasan ceased and pushed her from him.

But Prince Bhima cried out to the assembled princes and nobles, 'I call you to witness, O Princes and Nobles, that the day will come when I shall drink Prince Dushasan's life-blood as a vengeance for his cruelty.' But the evil Prince Duryodhan mocked Prince Bhima and said, 'And what wilt thou do to me for this, thou boaster?' As he spoke, he showed to the dark Princess his naked thigh. Prince Bhima's brow grew dark as Ganges, queen of rivers, when a squall lashes her to fury. 'Prince Duryodhan,' he cried, 'as surely as there are gods in heaven, I shall some day break in pieces with my mace the thigh which thou hast just now shown naked to the Princess Draupadi!'

The Princess Draupadi went to King Dhritarashtra's throne and knelt at his feet and said, 'O King, if thou wilt not give me justice, yet as an Aryan Princess, I have a right to ask of thee a boon. And the boon which I ask of thee is this. Free my husband Prince Yudhishthira from slavery.' And King Dhritarashtra said, 'Be it so, my child. As an Aryan Princess, I must grant thee a boon. I free thy husband Prince Yudhishthira from slavery.' Then the Princess Draupadi, still kneeling, said, 'O King, as an Aryan Princess, it is my right to ask of thee yet another boon, and the boon which I ask of thee is this. Free my husbands the Princes Bhima, Arjuna, Nakula, and Sahadev from slavery.' King Dhritarashtra said, 'Be it so, my child. As an Aryan Princess it is thy right to ask of me yet another boon. I free thy husbands the Princes Bhima, Arjuna, Nakula, and Sahadev from slavery. And wilt thou not ask of me yet another boon, that I should restore to thy five lords their wealth and their kingdom?' 'Nay, O King,' answered

Draupadi proudly. 'As an Aryan Princess it is my right to ask for two boons and no more. And as thou wilt not give me justice, I shall not ask of thee more than my right. My lords, too, once freed from bondage, will soon earn wealth and kingdoms for themselves.'

The old King's heart was softened when he heard the proud words of the Princess, and he said, 'Then, my child, I shall give thee a third boon without thy asking. I give back to thy five lords all that King Shakuni won from them. In return I would but ask that they cease to quarrel with my sons!' The hearts of the Pandavas were touched when they heard the old King's words, and, doing obeisance to their uncle, they and the dark Princess went back in their chariots towards Indraprastha.

But the curse of King Drupada would not let the anger of Prince Duryodhan die down in his heart. And when he saw that his father had freed the Pandavas from the net in which he had taken them, he grew well-nigh mad with grief and fury. Going to the King he said, 'Dost thou truly believe, O my father, that my cousins will forgive the wrongs that we have done them? Will Bhima forget his vow to drink Dushasan's blood or his oath to break my thigh with his mace? Even now the Pandavas must be calling their armies together in order to march on Hastinapura and destroy us all utterly.' Then King Dhritarashtra feared that, softened by Draupadi's words, he had acted rashly; so he replied, 'Thou speakest wise words, my son, but how shall we repair the fault that I have committed?' Duryodhan said, 'It is not yet too late, O my father. Let King Shakuni challenge Prince Yudhishthira to cast the dice just once more. And let the match be that the loser should give to the winner his kingdom and exile himself in the forest for twelve years and then disguise himself for one year more. If, during the thirteenth year, the winner pierce the loser's disguise, the loser shall be exiled for yet another twelve years.' The old King Dhritarashtra nodded assent. And a swift messenger rode after Prince Yudhishthira and came up with him near the gates of Indraprastha. 'Fair Prince,' said the messenger, 'King Dhritarashtra begs thee to return to his court and cast the dice once more.'

Prince Yudhishthira would willingly have refused to return. But the curse of King Drupada clouded his wits, and he thought that, as an Aryan Prince, he could not in honour draw back from a challenge. So he and his brothers and the dark Princess turned back with heavy hearts to the palace at Hastina pura. There King Shakuni said, 'My kinsman, thou hast regained thy wealth and I would not take it from thee again. But let our match be this. If thou winnest, Prince Duryodhan and his friends will go into exile for twelve years and then disguise themselves for one year more. And if the disguise is penetrated, they will go into exile for yet another twelve years. But if thou shouldst lose, thou and thy brothers will go into exile for twelve years and disguise yourselves for one year. And if the disguise is penetrated, you will go into exile for yet another twelve years.'

Prince Yudhishthira's friends cried, 'O Prince, have a care. Thou wilt surely lose to King Shakuni. But, prompted by the curse of King Drupada,' King Shakuni said in a mocking voice to the Prince, 'Thou dost well, my kinsman, not to risk the wealth that thou hast regained through King Dhritarashtra's charity.' Then once again the Prince's pride blazed up until it consumed all his wisdom, and he said, 'I am an Aryan Prince and I fear no risk. Let us throw the dice and let the stakes be as thou sayest.' The Prince and the King threw the dice, and when Shakuni looked at them, a glad smile spread over his cunning face. 'Indeed, my kinsman,' he cried, 'thy good fortune seems to have left thee for ever. For see! I have won again; and thou and thy brothers must now pay the forfeit.'

Prince Yudhishthira answered never a word. But he and his brothers clothed themselves in deerskins, and with nothing in their hands but their weapons they set out for the southern forests, that they might pass in them the twelve years of exile. And with them went the dark Princess of the Panchalas, who, in answer to King Drupada's prayers, had risen from the sacrificial fire to bring about the ruin of the Bharatas.

XII

BHIMA AND THE SERPENT

WHEN Prince Yudhishthira and his brothers and the Princess Draupadi left for the southern forests, a great multitude of the citizens of Indraprastha followed their rulers. And they wept and tore their hair and beat their breasts with grief. For they feared that the Pandavas would not endure the hard life in the southern forests and that they would die of fever or hunger before the twelve years had passed. Although Prince Yudhishthira often bade his subjects turn homewards, they followed him still, and night overtook them before they had started back to Indraprastha. So perforce they had to wait in the woods until the next morning.

When Prince Yudhishthira looked at the vast crowd that wept around him, his heart sank within him. For he had no food to give them, and without food they could not hope to walk back the many weary miles that parted them from Indraprastha. So he prayed to the sun-god, who had just sunk behind the tree-clad hills, to sustain his subjects until they reached their houses. And as he prayed, he said over the hundred and eight names by which men honour the sun-god. His prayer finished, he saw suddenly by his side a warrior clad in golden armour, which shone with such dazzling brilliancy that the Prince could not bear to lift his eyes towards it. For as the sun-god listened to the Prince's prayer, he bethought him of the sweet day when he had wooed and won Queen Kunti, still a maiden and unwed, and had by her become the father of Karna the charioteer. And as he thought, he felt pity for these her other sons. In an instant he had descended from the skies and was standing beside Prince Yudhishthira. 'O Bharata Prince,' said the dazzling sun-god, 'take this copper pot from me. In it thou shalt find enough and more than enough with which to feed this multitude.'

Prince Yudhishthira took the copper pot and gave it to Draupadi. And when she looked into it, she saw that it was full of food. She emptied it, but as soon as she emptied it, it forthwith filled again. And in this way she obtained, by pouring out time after time the contents of the inexhaustible pot, enough and more than enough with which to feed the citizens of Indraprastha. Refreshed by the food, they slept that night in the forest, and next day they rose and went sorrowing to their homes.

Yudhishthira and his brothers and the Princess Draupadi went ever farther into the southern forests. But Prince Yudhishthira was often plunged in thought. For he felt sure that, even if he kept the terms of the wager, and did not return to Indraprastha for thirteen years, the evil Prince Duryodhan would still not restore to him without bloodshed the kingdom and the wealth which he, Yudhishthira, had lost to King Shakuni. And the Prince thought of the many warriors who surrounded Duryodhan, all of the same mighty race as he himself. And he feared that he and his four brothers could never make head against them. One day there met him in the forest the ancient seer Vyasa, to whom King Drupada had referred the question of Draupadi's marriage. And the sage said, 'I know thee, O Bharata Prince, and I know, too, why thou wanderest wrapped in thought. Without the aid of the gods thou canst not prevail. But if the gods give thee celestial armour, thou mayest triumph. Send, therefore, thy brother Arjuna to the god Indra, who, so men say, is his father. And peradventure the god may bestow on Arjuna a coat of mail such as the Immortals wear. Wearing it, thy brother will, scatheless himself, shoot down with his myriad arrows the opposing hosts. Thus thou mayest conquer the evil Prince Duryodhan.'

These words of the ancient seer Prince Yudhishthira repeated to Prince Arjuna. And the latter cried, 'Gladly will I seek out the god Indra and beg him to give me celestial armour by which to conquer Prince Duryodhan when the years of exile and disguise are past.' So Prince Arjuna embraced his brothers and the dark Princess, and set forth alone towards the northern mountains. The road was long and weary from the southern forests to the Himalayas' snowy peaks. But the Prince was young and fearless, and day by day he walked northwards until one morning he saw, as he rose from sleep, the snow-clad peaks towering high above the fleecy clouds. Then he knew that he was nearing his journey's end. A day or two later he began to climb the mountain sides, and the rugged paths led him past foaming cascades and pine forests, through snow-drifts and over glaciers. But the stout heart of the Bharata Prince never failed him. He walked ever onwards towards Amravati, the celestial city, which the god Indra had built on the highest summit of the Himalayas.

One day as Prince Arjuna neared the topmost heights, he heard a voice cry to him, 'Stop!' He looked around and at last he saw a Brahman sage, who sat beneath a tree. Prince Arjuna went close to the sage to ask him why he bade him stop. But the sage said, 'O Bharata Prince, wherefore dost thou come with weapons and in armour to this abode of peace?' Prince Arjuna answered, 'Holy sir, I come not with weapons and in armour to do any man hurt, but that I may obtain celestial armour from the god Indra.' The sage replied, 'O Bharata Prince, when thou shalt see the greatest of all the Immortals, the god Shiva, face to face, then only shall the god Indra bestow on thee armour such as the Immortals wear.'

Prince Arjuna was about to ask how he should see the greatest of the Immortals, the god Shiva, face to face, when suddenly the Brahman ascetic vanished in the air, like a wisp of smoke in a light breeze. Prince Arjuna prostrated himself on the ground, for he knew that the sage with whom he had spoken could be none other than the god Indra whom he sought. Prince Arjuna journeyed no farther, but made his dwelling where he had seen the Brahman sage. And by night and day for many a weary month he ceased not to pray to the greatest of all the Immortals, the god Shiva, to reveal himself to him, Arjuna the Bharata, face to face.

One day Prince Arjuna left his hermitage to walk among the pine woods that grew all round it. As he walked a mighty boar rushed at him out of a neighbouring thicket. Swiftly came the boar, but swifter still the Bharata Prince fitted an arrow to his bow and shot the boar through the heart. Just as he had shot, another arrow hissed through the air and also pierced the boar's side. A moment later, a youth, clad in the dress of a mountaineer, stepped out of the woods and said, 'I have killed the boar, and I shall take it with me to my home.' Prince Arjuna looked at the young mountaineer and thought to himself, 'Never have my eyes rested on so beautiful a youth.' He was taller than are the sons of men. His skin shone with the radiance of an Eastern moon, and his eyes seemed to pierce to the Bharata's very heart. But Arjuna had the fierce pride of an Aryan Prince, and he could not brook that another should rob him of his quarry. 'If thou art wise, fair youth,' he said to the mountaineer, 'thou wilt go thy way. The boar is mine. And I, and not thou, shall bear it away to my dwelling-place.'

The mountaineer's brow grew dark as a stormy night, and he stepped forward as if to strike the Bharata. Prince Arjuna fitted an arrow to his bow and shot it straight at the young man's heart. But the arrow fell blunted at the mountaineer's feet. Prince Arjuna put his hand to his quiver to draw forth another shaft. But lo! the inexhaustible quiver, given him by the fire-god Agni, was empty. Nothing dismayed, Prince Arjuna rushed at the mountaineer to strike him down with the wood of his mighty bow. But the mountaineer with a laugh snatched the bow from the Bharata's hands. At last Prince Arjuna closed with his enemy, seeking to hurl him from the hill-top on which they stood. But although the Bharata's grip was fierce, that of the mountaineer was fiercer still. And in his awful embrace, the mighty strength of Prince Arjuna became that of a puny child. At last, all but crushed to death, he fainted and knew no more.

When he came back to life, he was lying upon the ground. In front of him he saw the mountainere still taller and more beautiful than before. Then Prince Arjuna knew that he with whom he had wrestled must be one of the Immortals. He lay on his face, touching the earth with his forehead, and said, 'Forgive me, I pray thee. I know now thou art one of the Immortals. For no man born of woman could have overcome me as thou didst.' Then a soft smile spread over the face of the tall mountaineer as he answered, 'O Bharata Prince! In answer to thy prayers, I have vouchsafed to thee what has hardly been vouchsafed to mortal man before. For I have given thee to see face to face the god Shiva, the greatest of all the Immortals.' Prince Arjuna looked upwards at the splendid youth and said: 'The god Indra promised me that, when I saw the god Shiva face to face, I should receive celestial armour against which the weapons of Prince Duryodhan and his warriors would be hurled in vain.'

But ere his words had ended, the mountaineer had vanished behind a hill, like the sun setting behind the mountain tops. Prince Arjuna, a moment later, looked around him. And lo! close at his side, he saw a suit of armour all of gold, yet so cunningly forged that in all of it there was not a single vulnerable spot. And such was its temper that no weapon forged by human hands could pierce it. He donned the armour, and it fitted perfectly his stalwart frame. He shouted and leapt with joy. For he felt his strength like that of an hundred men. And he knew that the god Indra had kept his word and had bestowed on him the celestial armour of the Immortals.

His task achieved, Prince Arjuna turned back from the snowy Himalaya peaks to the dark southern forests. For many a weary month Prince Yudhishthira and his brothers had vainly waited for Prince Arjuna's return. And latterly they had begun to mourn for him as one dead. But one day, as they sat together in a forest glade, they heard a footstep. Looking round, they saw coming towards them a man clad in armour of such dazzling radiance, that they had to shade their eyes with their hands before they could look at him. And Prince Yudhishthira said, 'Surely this stranger is no mortal man, but one of the gods. For never have I seen armour so splendid as that which he wears.' But the man answered with a laugh, 'Nay, Yudhishthira, it is but thy brother Prince Arjuna, who has come back to thee after many weary months, bringing with him the armour of the Immortals.' Then all the brothers rose to their feet and shouted with joy. And they clasped Prince Arjuna in their arms and rejoiced over him, as over one who had come back to them from the dead.

Then the five brothers and the dark Princess wandered together, as before, through the southern forests. But one morning Prince Bhima went out to hunt, and did not return. Towards evening the Princess Draupadi said to Prince Yudhishthira, 'Go thou forth and look for thy brother Bhima. I fear me that he has come by some ill. Else he would surely have come back ere this.' Prince Yudhishthira followed Prince Bhima's tracks through the forests, until they led him to a mighty cave. So dark and fearsome was the cave that, Bharata Prince though he was, Yudhishthira feared to enter. From outside he called to Prince Bhima. But he heard no answer save his own voice echoed back from the tree-clad hills. Then Yudhishthira tarried no longer. Drawing his sword he stepped inside the cave. When his eyes grew used to the light, he saw Prince Bhima lying almost lifeless within the coils of a mighty serpent. 'I wandered to this cave,' said Prince Bhima in a feeble voice, 'in search of game, for elsewhere I could find none. No sooner had I entered it, than this monstrous snake gripped me in its coils. For many an hour I have struggled with it. But now my strength fails, and unless thou canst free me, I die.'

Prince Yudhishthira spoke to the serpent softly and said, 'Fair serpent, he whom thou hast seized is prince Bhima, a king's son. If thou wilt but free him, I will give thee a noble ransom, and will bring thee all the food thou needest.' The mighty serpent answered nothing, but tightened its coils around the dying Bhima. Then Yudhishthira cried, 'As thou wilt not hearken to soft words, O serpent, then thou shalt suffer hard deeds. For I shall slay thee.' But the monstrous serpent laughed a hideous laugh and said, 'Of a truth, O Bharata Prince, thou hast little fear in thy heart, or thou wouldst not threaten me in my own den. But as thou at first didst speak me fair, I will give thee a chance of freeing thy brother. If thou answerest all the questions I ask thee, then I will set thy brother Bhima free But if thou failest to answer them, then I shall not only devour him but thee also.' 'Be it so, fair serpent,' answered Prince Yudhishthira, and awaited the monster's questions.

The serpent plied Prince Yudhishthira with questions on every subject—with questions touching on religion, on caste matters, on the holy books, on the laws, and on matters relating to government, to the duties of kings, and to the art of war. But no matter how dark the matter or how deep the question, the wise Prince Yudhishthira failed not to answer the serpent. For the gods had at his birth given Prince Yudhishthira power above all men to learn. And the great teachers who had taught him in his boyhood had instructed him in all the wisdom of the Aryans, which was far above that of other men. As the answer to the last question asked by the mighty snake passed Prince Yudhishthira's lips, the coils round Prince Bhima's body of a sudden vanished. Instead of the serpent there stood near the two Bharatas a man tall and of kingly bearing.

Prince Yudhishthira, with trembling voice, asked, 'Fair stranger, what does this mean? Who art thou? And where is the mighty snake which had coiled itself round my brother Bhima?' The tall stranger replied, 'O Bharata Prince, many hundred years ago I was King Nahusha of the great line of Ayu, sprung, like thine own line, from the loins of the moon-god. Over all the earth there was no king whose power was like mine. But such was my pride and foolishness that, instead of honouring Brahmans, I harnessed them to my palanquin and I made them carry it. One day I bade my guard harness to my palanquin the ancient sage Agasti. And because he was slow and weak with age, I struck him with my foot to make him go faster. Then the ancient sage Agasti called down on me a curse from heaven. And I was instantly turned into a monstrous, man-devouring snake. Then, in my fear and grief, I lay at Agasti's feet and begged him to free me from the curse. And he answered, "When there comes to thee a hero who can answer every question which thou shalt ask him, then only shalt thou be freed from my curse and become a man again." Now thou hast come, O Bharata Prince, and thou hast answered all my questions. So the sage's curse has fallen from me like a discarded garment.' And as the Princes gazed in wonder at the kingly stranger, he slowly ascended to the heavens, and they saw him no more.

XIII

THE YEAR OF DISGUISE

MONTH by month the twelve weary years of exile added themselves to each other and neared their end. And many adventures came to the Pandava Princes in the forest. But at last the twelfth year was complete, and they had to choose in which of the cities of India they should live disguised, and how they should disguise themselves, so that their concealment might not be pierced by the sharp-eyed spies of Prince Duryodhan. For everywhere he tracked the movements of the Pandavas, so that he might, when they had hidden themselves, penetrate their disguise and thus force them to suffer another twelve years of exile. After weighing in their minds the various cities of India, they at last resolved to live for a year in Viratnagar, the capital town of Virata, the kindly King of the Matsyas.

Now Prince Yudhishthira had during the twelve years of exile constantly practised dice-throwing, so that if King Shakuni challenged him again, he should not ruin the Pandavas as he had done before. In this way Prince Yudhishthira had become as skilled as King Shakuni himself. So when the dark Princess asked him what disguise he would take, he answered, 'I shall take the name of Kanka and shall put on the dress of a gambler.' Prince Bhima, who had, by cooking the food for himself and his brothers, become a skilled cook, said, 'I shall take the name of Ballaba and put on the dress of a cook.' Prince Arjuna, who danced and sang more skilfully than any mortal man, said, 'I shall take the name of Vrihannala and assume the guise of a dancer and singer.' Prince Nakula said, 'I shall take the name of Granthika and shall become a groom; for I love horses and can do a groom's work.' Prince Sahadev said, 'I shall take the name of Tantripala and become a cowherd; for from my childhood I have ever loved cattle, and shall not mind tending them.' Last of all the Princess Draupadi said, 'I shall take the name of

Sairandhri, and I shall disguise myself as a waiting-maid and tire-woman.' And when all the brothers and the Princess had settled what names and disguises they would take, they set out to the distant town of Virat-nagar, wherein ruled the kindly Virata, King of the Matsyas.

When they neared the city walls, Prince Yudhishthira said to Prince Arjuna, 'My brother, we should go no farther without hiding our weapons, else they will betray us, especially the Gandiva bow which the god Agni gave thee, and the golden armour which the god Indra bestowed on thee in the Himalayas.' Prince Arjuna replied, 'Wisely spoken, my brother. I see a burning-ground close to us. Let us hide our weapons and armour therein. For in a burning-ground none will care to search for them.'

Towards the burning-ground they went. In it there grew a mighty thorn-tree,* and Prince Arjuna said, 'Let us hide our arms and our armour in the thorn-tree.' The brothers in turn handed to Prince Nakula their weapons and their harness, and he tied them securely inside the branches of the thorn-tree. Now there happened to lie close to the tree the dead body of an old woman, which her kinsmen had borne to the burning-ground, but had been too undutiful to burn. Prince Nakula lifted it up and tied it also to the tree, so that passers-by might fear to look inside its branches. And to one or two passers-by, who had stopped to gaze at them, Prince Arjuna said, 'This is our old mother. It is the custom of our tribe to expose and not to burn our dead.' The passers-by, satisfied with his words, tarried no longer, but went their way.

Then one by one the Pandavas made their way to Virat-nagar. First Prince Yudhishthira asked for an audience with King Virata. And when the prince

* The particular thorn-tree is called a shami-tree.

entered the audience room, the King marvelled at his noble face and royal bearing and said, 'Who art thou, fair stranger, and why dost thou come to our city?' Prince Yudhishthira bowed low and said, 'O King, I am a Brahman, Kanka by name, and I am a skilled dicer. If thy days, 'O King, are weary, I shall beguile them. If thy nights, O King, are long, I shall make them pass swiftly.' King Virata's heart warmed towards the noble stranger, and he replied, 'O Kanka, thou must come to my palace and be my courtier. When the hours seem heavy, I shall call thee and we shall lighten them by casting dice together.'

A few hours later Prince Bhima entered the town gates with a cooking ladle and a spoon in one hand and a sword in the other. And he, too, asked for and obtained an audience with King Virata. The King wondered at the huge shoulders and thighs of Prince Bhima, and asked, 'Who art thou, fair stranger? From thy giant build I should say that thou art one of the heroes of Indraprastha. But thy garb is the garb of a cook.' Prince Bhima answered in humble tones, 'Nay, O King, I am no hero. I am but a cook, and my name is Ballaba, yet, if thou dost hire me as thy servant, thou wilt never regret it. For I surpass all men in the art of making curries and other delicacies.' So be it, Ballaba,' said King Virata, 'I take thee as my cook.'

Yet a few hours later there came to the main city gate the dark Princess of the Panchalas. Her dress was torn and soiled. Yet in spite of her rags, her beauty shone undiminished, and she looked more lovely by far than the fairest of the Matsya maidens. As Queen Sudeshna, King Virata's wife, drove through the city for her evening drive, she saw the beautiful Princess at the edge of the road. Queen Sudeshna bade her charioteer stay his horses so that she might speak with the lovely but ill-dressed woman, who stood by the roadside. 'Who art thou, fair girl?' asked Queen Sudeshna. 'Thou must be a stranger. For didst thou live always in Virata, I should surely have noticed thy beauty before.' 'O Queen,' said the dark Princess, 'thy words are true. I am a stranger, and my name is Sairandhri. I am a tire-woman, and I have come from a far country in search of employment. And if thou wilt take me as thy maid-servant, thou wilt never regret it. For I am the most skilled tire-woman in all India.' 'So be it,' said the kindly Queen. 'Go to my palace, and from to-night I take thee as my serving maid.'

Next day the King drove abroad to see his thousand kine that grazed along the meadows round Virata. In the meadows he saw a strange cowherd. He sent for him and he asked him his name. The cowherd replied, 'I come from Northern India, and my name is Tantripala. And if thou wilt but take me in thy service, thou wilt not regret it. For I am the most skilled of all the cowherds in India.' 'So be it,' said the kindly King. 'From to-day thou art one of my cowherds.' Thus, under the name of Tantripala, Prince Sahadev became King Virata's cowherd.

As King Virata's chariot bore him homewards, he saw near the city gate a man in a dancer's dress. The King thought that he had never before seen so noble a form and face. He said, 'Fair stranger, who art thou? and what dost thou in the dress of a dancer? Of a truth the gods made thy shoulders to bear armour and not to shake in time to a dancer's steps. For thou art more stalwart by far than any of my guardsmen.' The stranger said, with downcast eyes, 'O King, forgive me. I am no warrior and I know nothing of arms or armour, but I surpass all men in dancing and singing. If thou wilt hire me to teach dancing and singing to the ladies of thy house, they will soon surpass in skill the Gandharvas of Amravati.' 'So be it,' said King Virata. 'From to-day I hire thee to teach dancing and singing to my women-folk.'

Last of all King Virata went to his stables. Standing close to one of his horses, he saw a strange groom. 'Who art thou?' said King Virata. The groom replied, 'I am a groom, Granthika by name, and I seek service. To-day one of thy groom is dead, and I offer myself as thy servant in his stead. And if thou wilt take me as thy horse-tender thou wilt never regret it. For I shall care for thy horses as no other groom in India would.' 'So be it. Take the place of my dead groom,' said the King to the Prince Nakula. But after a moment he added sharply enough, 'But look to it that thy deeds equal thy words. For I love not idle boasters.'

Thus the five Pandavas and the dark Princess found various kinds of service with King Virata. And soon he grew to esteem them all greatly. For with Kanka the King passed merrily in dicing many hours which else would have passed with leaden feet. And the dinners cooked by Ballaba far surpassed those which the King's other cooks had prepared for him in the days gone by. Vrihannala, too, taught the King's ladies so skilfully to dance and sing, that he never grew weary of watching them or listening to them. And his kine grew from one to many thousands under Tantripala's fostering care. His horses never fell ill, so untiring was the service of the groom Granthika. While Queen Sudeshna vowed that in all India there was no tire-woman to equal her serving maid Sairandhri.

When twelve months had all but passed, there returned from a foreign war Queen Sudeshna's brother, Prince Kichaka. He was the bravest and fiercest warrior in all the wild lands of Virat-nagar. All men, even the kindly King himself, feared his savage temper and reckless daring. And all women feared to meet his gaze. For many a maid in Virat-nagar had lived to rue the day when his wicked eyes had first rested on her and found her fair. Prince Kichaka at once on entering the city did homage to King Virata. Next he went to see his sister Queen Sudeshna. As he talked to her, his eye fell on the lovely serving maid Sairandhri. And he begged Queen Sudeshna to send the maid to his palace. The Queen loved her brother so dearly that she could refuse him nothing. Sorely against her will, she bade Sairandhri make ready a tray of food and wine, and take it with her to Prince Kichaka's palace. Sairandhri said, 'O Queen, forgive me. I am thy tire-woman and I gladly do thy bidding. But I fear to go to Prince Kichaka's palace.' Queen Sudeshna, seeking to cajole her, said in a soft voice, 'Nay, fear not, fair Sairandhri. No one in Virat-nagar, not even my brother, would dare to wrong a serving maid from the King's palace.' Trusting the Queen's soft words, Sairandhri said, 'So be it, O Queen. I trust thee, and will take the tray of food and wine to Prince Kichaka's palace.'

Slowly and with sinking heart, the dark Princess set out with the tray to Prince Kichaka's palace. No sooner had she entered the door, than Prince Kichaka seized her by the waist and sought to embrace her. But the dark Princess freed herself lightly from his clasp, and, throwing in his face the tray of food and wine, fled back as fast as she could to King Virata's palace. Behind her, maddened with rage, Prince Kichaka ran swifter still. Overtaking her as she entered the palace door, he struck her face with his clenched fist. The Princess all but fell. Then recovering herself she fled straight on to the audience room of King Virata and burst into it unannounced. There she showed her bleeding face to the King and, telling him her story, cried aloud to him for justice. But King Virata feared to cross Prince Kichaka. He laughed at Draupadi and said to her lightly, 'Nay, I think thou thyself art the cruel one, fair waiting maid. Else thou wouldst never have left the Prince's love unrequited.'

The dark Princess answered nothing. Speechless with shame and anger, she slipped away from the audience room amid the laughter of the courtiers. She searched through the palace until she found Prince Bhima asleep in his room. She roused him and cried, 'My lord, shame on thee. Thou sleepest while thy wife suffers cruel wrong. Unless thou dost avenge me on Prince Kichaka, thou art no more husband of mine.' Then she told Bhima what had passed in Prince Kichaka's palace. The Pandava's mighty chest heaved with rage and his brow grew as dark as a northern winter, while he listened to her tale. 'Fear not, Princess of the Panchalas,' he said, holding out his huge hands. 'To-morrow night I will slay the monster with these. There is a dancing-hall in a distant part of the palace. Bid Prince Kichaka meet thee there to-morrow night. And I, instead of thee, will await his coming and he shall not leave my loving embrace alive.' The dark Princess smiled at the grim jest, and went away glad at heart.

Next morning she saw to it that Prince Kichaka should meet her. She looked at him from under her downcast lids and smiled. Kichaka thought that her anger had passed and that she wished him to renew his suit. He came near her and craved her pardon for his conduct on the previous day. Again the Princess looked at him and smiled.

Falling into her snare, he begged her to give him a meeting. Blushing, she whispered to him, 'Prince Kichaka, if thou wilt promise to keep our secret faithfully, I shall meet thee to-night in the dancing-hall in the distant part of the royal palace.' Prince Kichaka joyfully gave her his promise, and, filled with joy, he went his way.

That evening, as darkness fell, Prince Bhima went to the dancing-hall and hid himself there. And after everyone in the palace had gone to rest, he heard Prince Kichaka come tiptoe through the passage and enter the room. Through the darkness, Prince Kichaka saw a form in the room, and he thought that the waiting maid was before him at the tryst. 'Pardon me, fair maid,' he whispered, 'for my delay. For of a truth no maid hath ever moved my heart as thou hast.'

But as the words left his lips, Prince Bhima came close to him and whispered with a mocking laugh, 'Thou shalt love fair maids no more, valiant Prince, for I will so deal with thee to-night, that no maid shall know hereafter that thou ever wert a man.'

Prince Kichaka, although taken unawares, was a brave man and said, 'Who thou art, I know not. But it is easy to threaten. It is hard to perform.' Then both Bhima and Kichaka sprang at each other through the darkness. And they wrestled and fought up and down the dancing-hall and through the passage and back again into the dancing-hall. At last Prince Kichaka's strength, weakened by evil living, began to fail. Prince Bhima, seeing this, put forth his full force and threw Prince Kichaka on the ground. Kneeling on him, he gripped his throat with both his hands. Nor did he loosen his grip until Kichaka had ceased to breathe. Then, taking hold of his body, he kneaded it and pounded it, and rolled it up and down the floor until at last none could have said whether the body had been that of a man or of an animal.

When he had finished, the dark Princess came to his side. For, unknown to Bhima, she had followed Prince Kichaka, so that she might see his death. She smiled on Bhima and said, 'Well done, my lord. Thou hast made clean my honour and that of the Pandavas.' The Prince rose and embraced her and said, 'Draupadi, go thou and rouse the other maid-servants and say to them, "O serving maids, Prince Kichaka is dead. My husband, who is an Immortal, caught him with me. And, finding us together, my husband slew him."' The dark Princess went and roused the palace maids and said to them, 'O serving maids, what shall I do? I had a tryst with Prince Kichaka. My husband, who is an Immortal, caught us together and slew him.' The serving maids went back with Draupadi to the dancing-hall. And when they saw that nothing remained of Queen Sudeshna's brother but a shapeless mass of flesh, they said to Draupadi, 'Thy husband must indeed be an Immortal, for no man born of woman could have used the Prince so shamefully.'

XIV

THE END OF THE EXILE

THE serving maids told the death of Prince Kichaka to the palace guards. And by next morning all in Virat-nagar had heard that Prince Kichaka had been killed in King Virata's palace by the husband of the tire-woman Sairandhri. Prince Kichaka's kinsmen came to the palace and said haughtily to the King, 'For the sake of Sairandhri, O King, our kinsman Prince Kichaka lost his life. It is but right, therefore, that Sairandhri should burn with him on the pyre. The Prince and she will then, in the next world, enjoy their trysts unmolested.' The kindly King was loath to send Sairandhri to a cruel death, but he feared the kinsmen of the dead Prince. For they were many and powerful. Reluctantly he said, 'If it must be so, then take her with you and burn her to give rest to the dead Prince's spirit.'

When Sairandhri heard the King's answer, she said never a word. No tear dimmed her eye, nor did her cheek grow pale. For she was an Aryan Princess and scorned to show fear before the men of Virat-nagar. Proudly she walked towards the Prince's kinsmen and said, 'The King has spoken. As it is his will, take me and burn me on Prince Kichaka's pyre.' Prince Kichaka's kinsmen seized the dark Princess and bound her side by side with the dead man on his chariot of state. Behind the chariot the kinsmen, and after them a long line of warriors, followed with heads bowed. And from time to time they cast fierce looks of hatred at the tire-woman who, as they guessed, had led the Prince to his death.

Prince Bhima heard from outside the audience room King Virata's orders. Swiftly he left the palace. Swiftly he made his way by a lonely path to the burning-ground. From a tall tree which grew within it, he broke off a mighty bough, and fashioned it so as to serve him as a club. Then, hiding himself behind the tree, he waited until the chariot of Prince Kichaka should bear his body thither. Many weary minutes passed. At length he saw the head of the long procession coming towards him out of the distance. When the chariot had entered the burning-ground, and was come close to the tree, he uttered a fearful yell and rushed out from his hiding-place. Instantly the dark Princess cried joyfully, 'Lo! my husband, who is an Immortal, has come to set me free.' Taken unawares and unarmed, Prince Kichaka's kinsmen and soldiers fled panic-stricken on every side. But Prince Bhima followed them and struck one after another dead with his club. At last there was none left alive on the burning-ground, save only Prince Bhima and Draupadi. He came to her and loosed her bonds, and chafed her wrists and ankles where the cords had hurt them. Then he said to her, 'Walk back by the main road to Virat-nagar, I shall return by the lonely path by which I came.'

But in Virat-nagar all was confusion and dismay. Those of Prince Kichaka's kinsmen and soldiers who had escaped from Prince Bhima went crying through the city, 'Woe unto us, woe unto us! Sairandhri's husband, who is an Immortal, came upon us in the burning-ground and slaughtered us like sheep!' As they cried aloud, the dark Princess entered Virat-nagar. But all who saw her fled in terror, for they feared to be killed by her husband, who was an Immortal. Queen Sudeshna sent for the Princess Draupadi and said, 'Sairandhri, go where thou wilt, but stay not here. For the King fears alike the anger of thy husband and the vengeance of Prince Kichaka's kinsmen.' 'So be it. If thou biddest me, I shall go,' answered the dark Princess. 'But let me stay, I pray thee, for thirteen days more. Then I shall depart from Virat-nagar.' This she prayed because only thirteen days remained of the year in which they had to live disguised. And Queen Sudeshna granted her prayer.

Now when the news of Prince Kichaka's death reached the courts of the neighbouring Kings, they rejoiced greatly. For his valour had guarded Virat-nagar from the assaults of all foes. And, freed from the fear of his prowess, the neighbouring kings plotted to seize King Virata's kingdom. One day Susharma, King of the Trigarthas, who was a friend of the evil Prince Duryodhan, sent a herald to Hastinapura. 'Prince Kichaka is dead,' said the herald to Prince Duryodhan. 'And because of his death Virat-nagar lies an easy prey for the spoiler. Come, therefore, O Bharata heroes, and join your armies to those of King Susharma. Together we shall sack King Virata's cities and make his people our slaves.'

When the evil Prince Duryodhan heard the message, he rejoiced exceedingly. For he loved above all things to plunder the helpless and oppress the weak. So he said to the herald, 'Tell King Susharma that the Bharata heroes will go with him to the sacking of Virat-nagar. Let King Susharma raid King Virata's kine. And when King Virata's host pursues King Susharma to win back the kine, the Bharata heroes will fall upon Virat-nagar and destroy it utterly.'

As agreed, King Susharma, without declaring war, called out all his horsemen, and at their head he set out towards Virat-nagar. When they reached the meadows outside the city, they rode at the cowherds. They slew some and drove away the rest. Then, herding together King Virata's kine, they drove them away towards the lands of the Trigarthas. The cowherds who fled sought shelter in Virat-nagar. There, throwing themselves at the King's feet, they cried, 'Pardon, O King—pardon! We have lost thy kine, but we have in truth done no sin. A great band of horsemen rode at us and killed some and drove away the rest. But the kine they have carried off with them towards the lands of the Trigarthas.' King Virata grew very wroth. He bade his warriors don their armour and yoke their chariots. As soon as they were ready King Virata started to win back his kine from the Trigarthas. And in his army went Princes Yudhishthira and Bhima and Sahadev and

Nakula in their various disguises. All that day and night the Matsyas galloped after King Susharma's fleeing horsemen, and by noon next day came up with them. Then the horsemen fled no more. Suddenly turning, they furiously charged King Virata's warriors. Now, in the heat of the pursuit, these had scattered far and wide. So the horsemen slew them easily one by one. And in single combat King Susharma took King Virata captive.

Then Prince Bhima said to his brothers, 'The year of our disguise is over. Let us show these kine robbers the worth of the Pandavas.' At his words the four Bharata Princes rushed with a fierce battle-cry at the very heart of King Susharma's host. And beneath the mighty blows of Prince Bhima and the arrows of Prince Yudhishthira and the fierce sword-thrusts of Sahadev and Nakula, the Trigartha warriors fell like ripe wheat before the sickle. In the joy of triumph, Prince Bhima cried aloud, 'It is well for kine robbers to fight with cows. But against men they find it hard to stand.' Then, rushing at King Susharma's chariot, he caught him in his arms, and, lifting him as if he had been a child, the Prince bore the King captive to his own chariot. There he bound him tightly with cords. Seeing their King captive, the Trigarthas lost heart and fled in every quarter. King Virata, victorious and free once more, retook his cattle. And, extorting a great ransom from King Susharma, he went with his host in triumph to Virat-nagar.

Now, when King Virata had set out to pursue King Susharma, the evil Prince Duryodhan marched with a great force upon Virat-nagar, hoping to find it unguarded and to destroy it utterly. When the watchers on the city wall saw Prince Duryodhan's army nearing Virat-nagar, they fled in great fear to Prince Uttar, the eldest son of King Virata, whom the King had left in charge of his city. Now, Prince Uttar was unskilled in war and he was at a loss what to do. As he stood deep in thought, the tire-woman Sairandhri came near him, and said, 'O Prince, be not downcast. Take with thee Vrihannala the dancer. He will guide thy chariot against the host of Hastinapura And acting on his advice, thou shalt conquer Prince Duryodhan.'

Prince Uttar called to him Vrihannala, and with such troops as he could gather together, he set out to meet the army of Hastinapura. When he drew nigh and saw the great host before him and the few men with him, Prince Uttar's heart failed him. He said to his charioteer, 'Vrihannala, I pray thee turn my chariot and drive me with all speed to Virat-nagar.' But Vrihannala said, 'Nay, my Prince, flee not back to Virat-nagar. If thy heart faileth thee, take thou the reins and drive me towards the burning ground that lies outside the city.' Prince Uttar wondered greatly, but without a word he took the reins and drove the chariot to the burning-ground outside Virat-nagar. There he saw the skeleton of the old woman whom the Pandavas had tied to the thorn-tree. Dolefully it swung backwards and forwards in the wind. Then Vrihannala said, 'Go to the thorn-tree, my Prince, and fetch me the arms and armour tied inside its branches.' The Prince hesitated, for he feared the skeleton that swung backwards and forwards in the wind. Vrihannala laughed and said, 'Nay, Prince, fear not a dead woman's bones. Fetch me the arms as I bid thee.'

Slowly and with sinking heart Prince Uttar went to the tree and loosed the arms and armour and brought them to the chariot. Vrihannala donned the golden armour given him by the god Indra, and took in his left hand the Gandiva bow bestowed on him by the god Agni. And over his shoulders he fastened the inexhaustible quiver. So splendid did he look that Prince Uttar, with wide eyes and shaking voice, said, 'O Vrihannala, I thought thee but a dancing man. But of a truth thou must be the husband of Sairandhri, the Immortal who slew Prince Kichaka.' 'Nay, Prince,' laughed Vrihannala, 'I am no Immortal. I am only the dancer Vrihannala. Nevertheless, if thou wilt but drive the chariot against Duryodhan and his warriors, I shall make that evil Prince rue the day that he set out to plunder Virat-nagar.'

Cheered by the words of Vrihannala, Prince Uttar whipped his horses, and they drew the chariot with lightning speed back to the van of the Virat-nagar army. When King Virata's soldiers saw Prince Uttar driving his chariot against the foe, and beside him a warrior in golden armour, their spirits rose, and they stepped out gaily to meet the Hastinapura army. Then Vrihannala put his war-trumpet to his mouth, and he blew such a blast on it as had never before struck the ears of the Matsya people. A great cry of triumph rose from their lines and, breaking their ranks, they rushed headlong against the foe, even as the Ganges rushes to the sea when the summer sun melts the snows on the white peaks of the Himalayas. Once again Vrihannala blew on his war-trumpet, and Prince Uttar's horses galloped madly against Duryodhan's army. But when the Hastinapura warriors heard the blasts of the trumpet and saw the galloping chariot, in which stood the warrior in golden armour, and behind them the charging ranks of the Matsyas, their knees were loosened with fear. First the front line turned its back and then the line behind it. And in a few moments Duryodhan and his soldiers were swept away in headlong flight. The men of Virat-nagar followed them and slew them as they ran.

But out of the Hastinapura army a chariot shot forth to meet Vrihannala. The warrior in the chariot cried to him, 'I know thee, Prince Arjuna. I am Karna, the charioteer, whom thy dark Princess flouted on the archery ground of Panchala. To-day at least we shall see who is the better archer of us twain. Nor shall the dark Princess judge between us unfairly.' 'O valiant but base-born charioteer,' Prince Arjuna mocked him in reply, 'I thought that when I smote thee with my fist I had cured thee of thy wish to fight with men better born than thyself.' Karna bit his lips, but made no answer. The charioteers of the two warriors circled their chariots round each other. Suddenly Karna, seeing his chance, drew his bow swift as thought, and his arrow struck Prince Arjuna so fiercely on the chest that he well-nigh rolled upon the field. But the golden armour of the god Indra turned the arrrow-point, and it fell blunted to the ground.

'Indeed, thou hast some knowledge of archery,' cried Prince Arjuna, recovering himself, 'base born though thou art. But mayhap this will give thee still more knowledge.' Drawing the string of the great Gandiva bow to his ear, Prince Arjuna shot one of Varuna's arrows at Karna. The great shaft pierced through Karna's breastplate and would surely have cloven his heart. But his father, the sun-god, had pity on his son. He stopped the force of the arrow, so that it stayed its course and Karna died not. And his charioteer drove his horses so swiftly from the field that the Matsya horses toiled after Karna's chariot in vain. With Prince Duryodhan's flying army Karna's charioteer took his master back to Hastinapura, where the wise Aryan leeches cured him of his wound.

Then Vrihannala went back with Prince Uttar rejoicing to Virat-nagar, and the dancer's prowess was on all men's lips. When King Virata returned in triumph, he sent for Prince Yudhishthira and said, 'Tell me who you five men are, and why you have come to my town. For it is clear to me that you are all disguised.' Prince Yudhishthira replied, 'O King, we are the Bharata Princes, King Pandu's sons, whom the evil Prince Duryodhan robbed of their kingdom and drove away for thirteen years. But now the thirteen years are past and we wish to return to Indraprastha.' King Virata said, 'O Bharata Prince, had I known who thou and thy brothers were, I would have welcomed you as my sons. But let thy brother Arjuna, who has taught my daughters dancing, take one of them as his bride.' The King sent for Prince Arjuna and offered him his daughter, the Princess Uttara. But Arjuna said, 'O King, if I take thy daughter as my bride, evil men will say that I betrayed thy trust when I was her teacher. But I shall gladly take the maid, not for myself, but as the bride of my young son Abhimanyu, whom the Princess Subhadra of Dwarka has borne to me far away in Indraprastha.'

King Virata consented, and betrothed his daughter Uttara to Prince Arjuna's son Abhimanyu.

Then Prince Yudhishthira sent a herald to King Dhritarashtra at Hastinapura. The King received him in his assembly hall. And the herald said, 'O King, Prince Yudhishthira bids me tell thee that he and his brothers have passed twelve years in the forest and one year in disguise. And he asks thee to give him back his kingdom of Indraprastha.'

King Dhritarashtra took counsel of his son the evil Prince Duryodhan, and, following his false advice, he gave the herald a lying answer: 'Go tell Prince Yudhishthira and his brothers that the spies of Prince Duryodhan pierced their disguise before the thirteenth year was over. They must, therefore, under the terms of their wager, go into the forest for another twelve years.'

When the herald took the message back to Prince Yudhishthira, he grieved sorely ; for he wished not war, but peace. So he bade the envoy go once more to Hastinapura : 'Go tell King Dhritarashtra, herald, that if he will but give us five villages, one for each brother, we will take them and live peaceably under his rule.'

The herald went again to Hastinapura and gave the King Prince Yudhishthira's message. The old King would gladly have given his nephews the five villages. But his son the evil Prince Duryodhan whispered to King Dhritarashtra, 'Knowest thou not, O King, that if thou takest to thy bosom a frozen serpent, it will bite thee when revived by thy warmth ? Thy nephews speak now in humble tones and ask for but five villages, because they are ill and weak with hunger. Once they are revived with the yield of the five villages, they will plot as they did before to drive thee forth from thy kingdom.'

King Dhritarashtra said, 'Thy words are full of wisdom, my son. Let the frozen serpent die in the cold.' Then, turning to the herald, the King said, 'Go back to Prince Yudhishthira, herald, and bid him keep the terms of his wager. Until he has spent another twelve years in the forest, I shall not give to him or his brothers five villages, nay, nor even one village.'

So the herald went back sadly from Hastinapura and told Prince Yudhishthira the words of his uncle the King.

XV

THE GREAT BATTLE

WHEN Prince Yudhishthira heard King Dhritarashtra's message, his heart grew heavy. For he loved not bloodshed, and would gladly have forgiven even his evil cousin, Duryodhan. But he was an Aryan Prince, and his honour forbade him to suffer such wrong as that done by King Dhritarashtra. He turned to his brothers Arjuna and Bhima and said, 'You have heard, my brothers, the order brought us by the herald from the King. Falsely has the King said that Duryodhan's spies discovered us when at Virat-nagar. For if they had, our cousin would surely have proclaimed it aloud. What say you, then, my brothers? Shall we hark to King Dhritarashtra's unjust bidding, and spend another twelve years in the forest? Or shall we fight him, poor and friendless as we are, so as to win back our kingdom?'

Prince Arjuna looked at the dark Princess, and his eyes caught the angry flash of hers, as he answered hotly, 'Methinks, Yudhishthira, thou wouldst roam alone through the southern forests. For neither I, nor my brothers, nor the dark Princess, will serve thee there for another twelve years.' Then, drawing himself to his full height, Prince Arjuna cried in ringing tones, 'Have I not the Gandiva bow, O my brothers, and its inexhaustible quiver? Have I not Indra's golden armour, which the god of gods, Shiva, placed by my side on the peaks of the Himalayas? Nay, I promise thee, Yudhishthira, that I shall destroy in a single second all Duryodhan's army.' Prince Bhima laughed a mighty laugh as he smote Prince Arjuna on his wide shoulders. 'Bravely spoken, brother mine,' he said. 'But when thou destroyest Duryodhan's army, spare me, in thy mercy, Dushasan and Duryodhan. For I have vowed to drink Dushasan's blood and break Duryodhan's thigh!' The Princes Nakula and Sahadev said nothing, but their right hands gripped their golden sword-hilts, and their eyes gleamed fierce assent to the words of Prince Arjuna. Then Prince Yudhishthira sighed sadly and said, 'War, then, let it be, and let the guilt thereof rest on my evil cousin, Duryodhan.'

When Prince Yudhishthira told the kindly King Virata that he would make war on King Dhritarashtra, King Virata said, 'Take my soldiers with thee, O Prince, for they belong to thy brother Arjuna. Did he not save Virat-nagar from the hands of the spoiler? But do thou also send heralds to all the kings of India that we may have allies to help us fight against the evil Prince Duryodhan.' Prince Yudhishthira found the counsel wise, and he sent heralds to all the kings of India. And Drupada, King of the Panchalas, joined the Pandavas. For he knew, now, that the curse which he had called down on his foes would be fulfilled to the uttermost. And he went gladly to the battlefield that his eyes might feast on the slaughter of the Bharatas. And King Krishna, the wisest of all the Indian kings, sent word that he would go as Arjuna's charioteer. Some, too, of the Northern kings, who had loved the Pandavas aforetime, told the heralds that they would join Prince Yudhishthira. But most of the Aryan Princes, through fear of Prince Duryodhan, lent their hosts to him and not to the Pandavas. So when the armies met on the field of Kurukshetra, near Delhi, the Pandavas had but a small following. But the soldiers of Prince Duryodhan were many as the sands upon the seashore.

Now the Pandavas feared not the common soldiery, nor even the allied kings. But among Prince Duryodhan's army there were three heroes who could resist even the might of Prince Bhima, the archery of Prince Arjuna, and the valour of their brothers. The first and greatest was the wise old Prince Bhishma, the uncle of King Dhritarashtra. The river Ganges had borne him to King Shantanu. So he was the son of an Immortal.

And, old though he was, there was none braver or wiser than he in all Hastinapura. The second was Drona, who had taught Prince Duryodhan and his cousins archery and swordsmanship when they were boys together. The third was Karna, the sun-god's son and the greatest bowman, save only Arjuna, in all Northern India. So long as these three lived, victory inclined neither to one side nor to the other. And although the Pandavas slew many a gallant warrior of those who fought for Prince Duryodhan, his three heroes slew as many of those who fought for the Pandavas. And as the army of the Pandavas was far smaller than that of Prince Duryodhan, they felt the loss more than he did, and their army dwindled away daily, while his host seemed never to grow smaller.

At last, Prince Arjuna in despair stooped to a cruel trick, unworthy of an Aryan hero. There was in the army of the Pandavas a warrior called Shikhandi, who, good soldier though he was, wore always a woman's clothes. Prince Arjuna took him in his chariot and forced his way close to that of the wise old Prince Bhishma. From behind Shikhandi, Prince Arjuna showered arrows upon Prince Bhishma from his inexhaustible quiver. But Prince Bhishma, sore wounded though he was, would not shoot back, for he feared to wound Shikhandi, who, he thought, was a woman. And no Aryan Prince would willingly hurt a woman. Without retaliating, Prince Bhishma received the shafts from Arjuna's inexhaustible quiver, until at last he sank to the ground. But so thickly covered was he with arrows that no part of his body could touch the earth. So he lay on the arrows as if on a couch. And, indeed, no couch could have been fitter for an Aryan hero of those days.

At length, weary with years and pain, Prince Bhishma's spirit longed to be free. But the sun was still in its southward course. And it was deemed unseemly that an Aryan hero should die while the sun was in its southern course. So Ganges, the mother of Prince Bhishma, and queen of all rivers, sent from the Manas lake in far Thibet, near which she has her source, a flock of wild swans to Prince Bhishma. Just as the Prince was about to close his eyes in death, he saw the wild swans like specks on the northern horizon. Nearer and nearer they came until they reached the spot where Bhishma lay. Then they circled round the dying hero, and their leader cried, 'It is not seemly that Prince Bhishma should die until the sun has turned northwards.' When the Bharata warrior heard these words, he, with a mighty effort, held his spirit back and said, 'Well spoken, wild swan from the north; I shall not suffer my spirit to go free until the sun turns northwards towards the ecliptic.'

When the soldiers in both armies heard Prince Bhishma's words, they prostrated themselves before one whose spirit neither age nor death could tame. And by common consent they called a truce until the hero should suffer his soul to go free. Round his body they dug a trench, so that wild beasts should not harass him. And Prince Arjuna came near to him and said, 'Prince Bhishma, I played a cruel trick on thee, and I crave thy pardon.' The ancient hero answered, 'Nay, Prince Arjuna, I forgive thee freely. For although thou hast acted in a way unworthy of the great Bharata line, yet thou hast had the courage to own thy fault. But have a care, I bid thee. For the Immortals are angry with thee for the trick which thou didst play on me.'

After a few moments, Prince Bhishma added, 'Prince Arjuna, thy arrows bear my body a foot above the earth. But my head hangs down and I need a pillow.' Prince Arjuna answered, 'I shall make ready for thee a pillow worthy of a dying Bharata.' With these words he shot three arrows into the ground, so that their feathered butts came out just below Prince Bhishma's head, and he could rest his head upon them. 'I thank thee, Prince Arjuna,' said Prince Bhishma. 'Now bring me some water, for I am thirsty.' 'Whence shall I bring it?' asked Arjuna. 'For there is no stream at hand.' 'Shoot thy arrow into the earth at the spot which I shall show thee,' said Prince Bhishma, and he pointed to a hollow a few yards away. Prince Arjuna shot his arrow into the hollow, and up there spouted a stream of clear, cool water which Ganges, queen of rivers, had sent underground to her dying son. Prince Arjuna filled his helmet with water, and Prince Bhishma drank it greedily. 'Now I am at ease,' said Prince Bhishma, 'and I can wait in peace until the sun goes northwards.'

Then all the warriors came and spoke with him and asked his counsel, and to all who asked him he gave answers that were pearls of wisdom. Thus day by day the time went on. At last the hour came when the sun turned northwards; Prince Bhishma[1] closed his eyes and let his spirit go free. The god Indra threw wide the doors of his heaven. And all the Immortals who dwelt within it greeted the Bharata hero with acclamation.

After Prince Bhishma's death, the warriors in the two armies again took up their arms and, as before, victory inclined sometimes to Duryodhan and sometimes to the Pandavas. Now there was in Prince Yudhishthira's army, Prince Dhrishta-dyumna, the son of King Drupada. And he longed to make clear his father's honour by killing the hero Drona, who with the Bharata Prince had overcome the Panchalas. So, driving his chariot close

1 See Appendix B.

to that of Drona, Prince Dhrishtadyumna called out, 'Thy son Ashwathama is slain. Hast thou not heard of it, O Drona?' Drona said, 'I have not heard of my son's death, nor do I now believe thee. For there never yet was a Panchala who was not false to his word. But I shall ask Prince Yudhishthira.' Driving his chariot towards Prince Yudhishthira, Drona said, 'Tell me, O Prince, is Ashwathama dead or living? For I trust thy word against all men.'

Now just before Drona had asked the question, an arrow from one of Duryodhan's soldiers had struck Prince Yudhishthira's favourite elephant, and its name also was Ashwathama. So Prince Yudhishthira, thinking that Drona spoke of the elephant, answered, 'Yes, O Drona, Ashwathama is dead.' Then Drona believed that his son had been killed. He let his weapons fall from his hands, and with them he covered his face. For he loved his son Ashwathama better than life itself. The false Dhrishtadyumna, seeing Drona helpless with grief, rushed at him and with his sword smote him where the corselet meets the helmet. The sword shore clean through Drona's neck, so that his head fell off and rolled in the dust close to his chariot wheel. But when Prince Yudhishthira learned the lie which the Panchala Prince had uttered, the Bharata grieved exceedingly. And he said to his brother Arjuna, 'What will it avail us to win our kingdom, for we have stained the honour of the Bharata heroes?'

On Drona's death Prince Duryodhan gave to Karna, the sun-god's son, the command of all the army. And, rejoicing at the honour conferred on him, although by caste only a charioteer, Karna surpassed all his former acts of valour. Everywhere his chariot passed its track could be followed by the heaps of dead who lay stricken by his arrows. At length Prince Yudhishthira called to his brother Arjuna, 'Go thou and seek out Karna and, if thou canst, destroy him. For unless he dies, we shall not when night falls have a warrior left.'

Prince Arjuna bade his charioteer the wise King Krishna of Dwarka seek out the chariot of Karna, so that he, Arjuna, might fight Karna to the death. When Karna became aware that Prince Arjuna sought him, he gladly told his charioteer to turn his horses and face the foe. Round and round each other the chariots circled, each archer seeking for a chance whereby he might shoot his enemy. So skilful was the wise King Krishna that Prince Arjuna's chariot never checked its speed, and Karna could not take sure aim. But Karna's charioteer by mistake drove his horses into a ditch by the roadside, so that the chariot stopped. The same moment Prince Arjuna's arrow left his bow, swift as thought, and piercing Karna's breastplate clove his heart in two. When the sun-god saw his son fall, he grieved sorely. And his tears fell as soft cooling rain, which refreshed the warriors who fought on the field of Kurukshetra. In this way died the third great hero who fought for Duryodhan.

But when Prince Duryodhan's hosts learned of the fall of the hero Karna, a great panic seized on them and they fled to every quarter of the field. But no matter where they fled, the Pandavas followed and slew them without ceasing. And Prince Bhima overtook Prince Dushasan as he ran, and hurling him to the ground, tore open his chest and drank from it his heart's blood. For even so Bhima had vowed to do thirteen years before in the palace at Hastinapura. And when night fell, there remained alive out of that mighty host, only Duryodhan himself and Ashwathama the son of

Drona and two of his companions, who had fled with him. They were named Kripa and Kritavarman.

XVI

DURYODHAN'S DEATH

WHEN next morning the sun rose, the Pandavas searched every spot on the battlefield, hoping to find the dead body of the evil Prince Duryodhan. For they knew that, so long as he lived, they would never hold their kingdom in peace. Now in old times a wizard had built for the evil Prince Duryodhan a wondrous magic palace at the bottom of the lake Dwaipayana. And when Prince Duryodhan fled from the slaughter of the previous day, he thought it safe to seek a hiding-place in the wizard's palace. When he came to the edge of the water, he repeated softly the charm which the wizard had taught him, and on each side the water of the lake retreated, leaving the evil Prince a dry path along which to pass to his palace. When he had entered it, he closed the outer door and once more spoke softly the charm. Instantly the waters united and hid all trace of the path. Thus no matter where the Pandavas sought for Duryodhan they failed to find him. But Ashwathama, Drona's son, knew of the magic palace, and he guessed that Duryodhan had hidden himself there. So he came to the edge of the lake and called to Duryodhan, and Duryodhan's voice answered him from the depths of its waters.

Now it chanced that some hunters, in quest of food for the Pandava army, were passing close to the lake. They heard the voice of Duryodhan rise from its depths and answer Ashwathama, the son of Drona. They carried the news to Prince Yudhishthira and his brothers and then guided them and the wise King Krishna to Lake Dwaipayana. When the Pandavas came to the edge they called to Prince Duryodhan, and he mocked them from his magic palace at the bottom of the lake. Prince Bhima in a fury said he would plunge into its waters and drag his evil cousin to the shore and then slay him. But Prince Duryodhan uttered softly another charm which the wizard had taught him, and the waters of the lake turned to solid crystal, so that Prince Bhima could not plunge into them. And the more the Pandavas railed at Prince Duryodhan, the more he mocked them. 'Nay, fair cousins,' he said, 'I am but one and you are five; why, then, should I leave my magic palace to be killed by you in unfair fight? If Yudhishthira were to promise that only one of you would fight me at a time, then gladly would I leave my magic palace and fight you one after the other on the shores of the lake.'

Then a noble thought came to Prince Yudhishthira, and he cried to his cousin, 'Fair cousin, if thou art really a Bharata Prince, thou wilt accept the challenge which I now offer thee. Come from thy magic palace and choose whom among us thou wilt fight and with what weapon. If thou shouldst conquer the foe chosen by thee, I will resign to thee the kingdom and all my claims without further bloodshed. If thou art conquered, thou shalt resign to us the kingdom and all thy claims.' Prince Duryodhan, evil though he was, was yet no coward. He gladly accepted his cousin's challenge. 'I trust thy word, fair cousin,' he said, 'and I come forth from my magic palace. I choose Prince Bhima as my foe and the mace as our weapons.' Prince Arjuna was aghast when he heard his brother risk all that they had won in the mighty battle. But Prince Bhima said: 'Fear not, my brother. I shall break in pieces Duryodhan's

THE MACE FIGHT BY THE LAKE

thigh with my mace, even as I vowed to do when, to insult Draupadi, the dark Princess, he bared it before her in the palace at Hastinapura.'

Now all the years during which the Pandavas had been exiled in the woods and had hidden themselves in Virat-nagar, Duryodhan had daily practised with his mace. So that in all India there was none now so skilled as he in mace-play. Thus he hoped easily to overcome Prince Bhima. Softly he uttered the magic charm, and the lake's hard crystal turned again to sparkling water. Softly he uttered the second charm, and on each side the waters of the lake retreated, leaving a dry path between. Along the path Prince Duryodhan walked, mace in hand, from the magic palace to the shore. Then with a cry of fury he rushed at Prince Bhima. Up and down the banks of Lake Dwaipayana the fight raged. And many a cunning mace trick Prince Duryodhan displayed. Many a time the blows passed through Prince Bhima's guard. The blood poured in streams down his mighty chest and neck. And many a time his brothers wrung their hands in agony; for they thought that he would fall under Duryodhan's cunning blows. But although Prince Bhima was less skilled in mace-play, yet the heart within him was unyielding. Although the mace blows rained on him, Prince Bhima bore them patiently, sure that sooner or later his chance would come.

At last Duryodhan, thinking that his foe was exhausted, rose to his full height to deal a blow which would break Bhima's skull to fragments. But as Duryodhan did so, he unguarded his thigh. And Prince Bhima, seeing that his chance had come, swung his mace at it with all his force. And beneath that mighty stroke Prince Duryodhan's thigh-bone was broken in pieces, just as Prince

Bhima had foretold thirteen years before in the palace of King Dhritarashtra. Prince Duryodhan fell to earth and the fight ended. After tending him as best they could, the Pandava Princes returned next morning to their camp. There a fearful sight met their eyes. Of all the Pandava warriors who had survived the battle of Kurukshetra, not one remained alive. Everywhere their dead bodies lay strewn inside the tents or along the paths between them.

When Ashwathama and his two companions, Kripa and Kritavarman, learnt that the Pandavas had left their camp to seek out Duryodhan, they plotted a fearful deed. At the dead of night they went to Dhrishtadyumna's tent and slew him as he slept. And as Ashwathama gripped Dhrishtadyumna by the throat he muttered, 'Now thou canst learn, thou false Panchala, whether I am dead as thou didst tell my father Drona, or not.'

From Dhrishtadyumna's tent the slayers went to the other tents in turn and slew all their inmates. Nor did any one try to hinder them. For the gods were, as Prince Bhishma had said, angry with Prince Arjuna for the cruel trick which he had played on the son of Ganges, queen of rivers. And the curse called down by King Drupada would not suffer their anger to die down in the hearts of the gods. So they wrapped Prince Yudhishthira's warriors in a slumber so deep that the screams of their comrades could not rouse them. Thus one by one Ashwathama and his two companies slew the whole Pandava army save only Yudhishthira and his brothers and the wise King Krishna. Ashwathama's work complete, he and his companions went back to the shore of Lake Dwaipayana where Prince Duryodhan lay. The evil Prince was in great pain. And after the Pandavas had left him, wolves and hyenas had gathered round him and strove to devour him while he still lived, and he kept them off with ever-increasing difficulty. Ashwathama drove away the wild beasts and, drawing near to the dying Duryodhan, told him how he had slaughtered the Pandavas as they slept. A smile of triumph lit up the Bharata's face. 'Living,' he murmured, 'I robbed them of their crown. Dying I have robbed them of victory.' But as the words left his lips, the smile faded and the soul of King Dhritarashtra's son freed itself from its earthly mansion.

In this way the curse was fulfilled which King Drupada had called down on the Bharatas. For Prince Arjuna's son Abhimanyu had been killed by Lakshman, son of Duryodhan, in the battle. And the sons whom Draupadi the dark Princess had borne to her five lords had all been slaughtered by Ashwathama as they slept. All King Dhritarashtra's hundred sons were dead, and so too were all his kinsmen except his five nephews. But as neither he nor they had any offspring, it was clear that the great Bharata line must in a few years be extinguished for ever.

After the Pandavas had sorrowed over the slaughter of Draupadi's sons and of their army, they and the wise King Krishna went to Hastinapura. When King Dhritarashtra heard of their coming, he went to the palace gate to meet them. He first embraced Prince Yudhishthira, but coldly, for he loved him not. Then he put forth his arms to embrace his nephew Bhima. But the Prince had stepped aside while Prince Yudhishthira and the King greeted each other. And it was well for him that he had done so. For the blind old King put his hands out until they touched an iron statue. Then, thinking that they touched his nephew, King Dhritarashtra locked his arms round it and squeezed it with such fearful force that, had Bhima entered the King's embrace, he would never have left it alive. For before the King's grip relaxed, the iron statue fell to the ground, broken into tiny pieces.

'Methinks, my uncle,' growled Prince Bhima, 'if that is how thou greetest thy nephew whom thou lovest, I had sooner be counted among thy foes.'

But the old King heard not his nephew's words. Exhausted by the supreme effort, he fainted, and was carried back inside the palace.

Prince Yudhishthira, however, never lessened his courtesy to King Dhritarashtra. He ordered all men, including his brothers, to treat his uncle as still King of all Hastinapura, under pain of his severe displeasure. He ordered, too, that all honour should be paid to the spirits of the Bharatas who had fallen in the war, whether they had fought for him or for Duryodhan. But he grieved sorely for the end of the Bharata line, which, as he saw, was at hand. And he prayed to the Immortals and told them all his sorrow. And the kindly gods pitied him, and they stayed the curse which King Drupada had called down from heaven on the Bharatas.

Now King Virata, at Prince Arjuna's bidding, had given to his son Abhimanyu his daughter the Princess Uttara. The marriage had been celebrated, and they had lived happily together before the young Prince had fallen in battle. And one day when Prince Yudhishthira grieved for the mighty Bharata line, a serving maid brought him the joyous news that the Princess Uttara had borne to her dead lord a baby boy. Then right glad was the Prince Yudhishthira. And right glad were his brothers when he told them. Right glad, too, were all the citizens of Hastinapura. For they loved loyally the great Bharata Kings who had ruled over them for so many generations. And Prince Yudhishthira gave the child the name of Parikshit.

For after the Bharata line had come to an end, he gave it fresh life.

For fifteen years King Dhritarashtra continued to rule over Hastinapura. And always Prince Yudhishthira served him faithfully, so that the old King grew to love his eldest nephew as if he had been his own son. So, too, the Princes Arjuna, Nakula, and Sahadev did the old King faithful service. But Prince Bhima never forgave King Dhritarashtra for the treacherous embrace in which his uncle had sought to take his life. And though he honoured Prince Yudhishthira too much to speak in his presence unkindly to their uncle, yet, whenever his eldest brother was away, Prince Bhima used to rebuke King Dhritarashtra and his wife Queen Gandhari for all the grief and misery which their son Duryodhan had brought on the kingdom. One day in the old King's presence Prince Bhima slapped his mighty arms and said, 'These, O King, are the arms with which I slew thy sons, and especially the evil Prince Duryodhan.' King Dhritarashtra answered not a word, but he bowed his head in grief, as he thought of his hundred sons, who had grown around him from childhood to boyhood and from boyhood to manhood, but who were now no more.

When King Dhritarashtra's grief had abated, he sent for Prince Yudhishthira. 'O Prince,' he said, 'when an Aryan King feels death drawing nigh, it is his custom to resign his kingdom and enter the forests, there to greet death as a friend, when it comes. And I am weary with life and would welcome death. I wish to resign to thee the burden of rule and go with Queen Gandhari into the forests.'

Prince Yudhishthira did his utmost to turn the aged King from his resolve, but in vain. He and Queen Gandhari, amid the tears of the citizens, left

Hastinapura for the forests. And with them went Queen Kunti. For she, too, was weary of life and sorrowed always for her gallant son, Karna the charioteer, whom she had borne to her lover the sun-god. Then King Dhritarashtra and the two Queens lived as hermits in a forest glade near the banks of the Ganges.

One day there arose a forest fire. Fanned by a strong north wind, it encircled the glade where the aged King dwelt, so that there was no escape. He turned his face to the east, whence every day rose the life-giving sun. Then, casting aside all fear, he and the two Queens waited for the flames to consume them and free them from their ceaseless sorrow. Nearer and nearer the flames came, and great tongues of fire shot past them and burnt the grass round them in an ever-narrowing circle. Suddenly the wind blew a mass of burning trees across their bodies as they sat, so that in a moment they were enveloped in the flames. But never a murmur escaped the lips of any of the three. At last all that remained of them was a heap of ashes. In this way died King Dhritarashtra of the great Bharata line. And when the news of his death reached Hastinapura, Prince Yudhishthira, the son of Pandu the Bharata, was crowned King in his stead.

XVII

THE DEATH OF KING KRISHNA

FOR twenty years after the death of King Dhritarashtra, his nephew ruled wisely and justly over the kingdom of Hastinapura. In these happy years the rain fell at the appointed seasons and famine was unknown in the land. Never before had the citizens of Hastinapura been so happy and prosperous as under the rule of King Yudhishthira the Bharata. But when the twenty years had passed, a great grief came to sadden the King and his four brothers: to wit, the death of the wise King Krishna of Dwarka.

In early manhood the wise King Krishna had been one of the greatest heroes in all India, and indeed men whispered that he was the great Lord Vishnu incarnate. His father was Prince Vasudev, the son of Shursena, King of the Yadhavs and brother of Qneen Kunti. His mother was the Princess Devki, the cousin of a very wicked ruler, King Kansa of Mathura. Now at the marriage of Krishna's parents, King Kansa had heard a voice call from the sky: 'To-day King Kansa honours her whose eighth child will slay him.' And because of these words, King Kansa had slain Devki's first six children. But the seventh and eighth child escaped his wrath. They were taken by stealth from Mathura to Gokula, and brought up as the children of Nanda the cowherd. And they were named Balarama and Krishna.

At Gokula they were beyond King Kansa's jurisdiction, but when he came to learn where they were hidden, he was untiring in his efforts to destroy them. Once he sent a female demon, Putana by name, to suckle the children with her poisonous milk. But Krishna drew from the demon nurse not only her milk but also her life-blood. When Krishna grew to manhood, King Kansa sent to slay him a mighty bull called Arishta, and a man-killing horse called Keshi. But Krishna sprang on the bull's back, and tearing out its left horn beat out the beast's brains with it. When Keshi rushed at Krishna open-mouthed, he seized its tongue and tore it out.

At last King Kansa invited Krishna and his brother to a wrestling match, hoping that the royal wrestlers would conquer and slay his two young kinsmen. But they threw the royal wrestlers on the ground and killed them one after the other. Then leaving the wrestling-ground, Krishna rushed at the royal seat, dragged King Kansa from it by the hair, and slew him in the arena. Krishna placed on the throne in Kansa's stead his brother Ugrasena. And he and Balarama went away to the shore of the western sea and there founded the beautiful city of Dwarka. And years afterwards when the Pandavas' herald told King Krishna that they were marching on Hastinapura, he joined them and served through the battle of Kurukshetra as the charioteer of Arjuna, who had wedded Subhadra, Krishna's sister.

Now when the mighty battle was over, King Krishna took leave of Prince Yudhishthira and ruled for thirty-five years over the Yadhavs and the Vrishnis, who were his subjects. And just as the citizens of Hastinapura enjoyed great wealth and prosperity under King Yudhishthira, so the people of Dwarka were happy and rich under the wise King Krishna. But one day some nobles of the wise King mocked the mighty seer Vishvamitra. He called down from heaven a fearful curse upon the townspeople of Dwarka. And he foretold that they should all die at one another's hands. When the wise King Krishna heard of the curse, he thought to himself: 'Men only fight with each other when drunk with wine. If I forbid wine in Dwarka, I may yet avert the curse.' So the wise King Krishna issued an order that no one should prepare in the city or bring into it any intoxicating drink, and he proclaimed that he would impale anyone who disobeyed his order.

One day one of King Krishna's Queens said to him, 'Last night, O King, I had a fearful dream. I saw a woman with black skin and huge white teeth enter all the houses in Dwarka and tear from the women's wrists the threads which show that their husbands are still living. Then the dream changed. And I saw a band of vultures descend on the houses and devour the bodies of all the men in Dwarka'.

King Krishna thought that the gods must have sent his Queen this dream as a sign of their anger. He ordered all the townsmen in Dwarka to go with him to the edge of the sea and there worship the Immortal gods. But once outside the walls of Dwarka, the townsmen no longer heeded King Krishna's ordinance forbidding wine. They and the King's soldiers bought wine and drank it greedily. As they had abstained from it for many years, it soon darkened their minds. They began to exchange with each other sharp words. And from words they soon passed to blows. And in a few hours there was not a single male left alive out of all the townspeople of Dwarka. Then the wise King, distracted with grief, sent to Hastinapura a messenger, by name Daruka, to tell his kinsmen the Pandavas of the slaughter of his townsmen. While waiting for Daruka's return, King Krishna and Balarama went into the forest, hoping to appease the Immortals by their penances. But as they sat together Balarama, weary with grief and years, let his spirit go free.

So the wise King Krishna sat alone in the deep forest and thought of all the stirring deeds of his early life and of the great battle in which the Bharata heroes had slaughtered each other. So motionless he sat, that a hunter, Jara by name, who chanced to be tracking deer, thought that King Krishna was a stag asleep. Drawing his bow until the feathers of the arrow touched his ear, the hunter Jara let the bow-string fly. So true was the aim that the arrow-head entered King Krishna's heel. Seeing that he had hit his mark, Jara ran to the spot to seize his quarry. When he came close he saw that it was no stag that he had wounded, but the wise King Krishna of Dwarka. The hunter threw himself at his lord's feet in an agony of fear and grief and begged his forgiveness. But no word did King Krishna answer him. Far away, as if in a dream, he saw the white, cool peaks of the Himalayas. And he longed to be free from this world of pain and sorrow and see again Balarama and Queen Kunti and the mighty Bharata heroes, who had fallen on the field of Kurukshetra. The Immortals took pity on the dying King, and they sent earthwards the kindly messengers of death, who softly led King Krishna's soul from its earthly tenement to the god Indra's heaven.

When Daruka the messenger reached Hastinapura and told of the slaughter of King Krishna's subjects, Prince Arjuna said, 'Gladly shall I go to Dwarka and comfort my kinsman the wise King Krishna. For it was by his skill as a charioteer that I overcame Karna's archery.' But when Prince Arjuna reached Dwarka, he learnt that the wise King Krishna had died also. So Prince Arjuna could but give honour to his shade with rites worthy of an Aryan hero. When King Krishna's body was laid on the funeral pyre, four of his wives threw themselves on his corpse, and thus purified by the flames, joined him in heaven. But Prince Arjuna called together the other women of King Krishna's household, and set forth with them to Hastinapura. As they started they saw a mighty wave form far away at sea and swiftly approach the seashore, just as if a mountain were moving over the face of the waters. When the wave met the shore, so vast was it that it stopped not, but spread over all Dwarka, the city of King Krishna, and destroyed it utterly. And to this day men point from the coast of Kathiawar to a spot far out at sea where King

Krishna's city stood in the days of the Bharata heroes.

After the sea had swallowed up Dwarka, Prince Arjuna went northwards with the women of King Krishna's household. All went well until he reached the land of the five rivers, which men to-day call the Punjab. There a countless horde of robbers and barbarians flung themselves on Prince Arjuna and his escort. Prince Arjuna, in the pride of his former deeds, called to them, 'Barbarians, you are but rushing to your own death.' But they heeded him not. Swiftly he fixed an arrow to the Gandiva bow and thought soon to shoot down the barbarian horde with the shafts of his inexhaustible quiver. But, although he knew it not, the years had slowly robbed him of the strength that had made him the first of Indian archers. And when he strove to pull the bowstring his weakened arms tugged at it in vain. So the barbarians fell upon Krishna's women and led them away into captivity.

Sadly Prince Arjuna made his way to Hastinapura and told King Yudhishthira the evil things that had happened. The King sorrowed much for the wise King Krishna and for his subjects. But when he heard what had befallen Prince Arjuna, and that his arm could no longer bend the Gandiva bow, he remembered the words of King Dhritarashtra: 'When an Aryan King feels death drawing nigh, it is his custom to resign his kingdom and enter the forests, there to meet death as a friend, when it comes.' He repeated them to Prince Arjuna and said, 'My brother, the time has come for us to observe the custom of the Aryan Kings. Let us therefore leave Hastinapura and go to meet death as a friend, and not wait for it here.' And Prince Arjuna and the Princes Bhima, Nakula, and Sahadev readily assented.

King Yudhishthira called to him Prince Arjuna's

grandson, the Prince Parikshit, whom the Princess Uttara had borne to her gallant husband Abhimanyu, after he had fallen on the battlefield. Then taking from his own head the crown of Hastinapura, King Yudhishthira placed it on the head of his great-nephew. He took up the robes of state and laid them on Prince Parikshit's shoulders. Then calling together his counsellors, he ordered them to issue throughout the length and breadth of the mighty Bharata kingdom this proclamation:

'King Yudhishthira has resigned the diadem of Hastinapura, and King Parikshit, the son of Abhimanyu, the son of Arjuna the Bharata, has been crowned King in King Yudhishthira's stead.'

Then the five brothers and Queen Draupadi sacrificed to the immortal gods, and after the gods had been gladdened by the sacrifice, King Yudhishthira clad himself in garments of bark and deer-skins, so that he resembled one of the tribesmen who dwelt in the wild southern forests. His brothers and Queen Draupadi did likewise. King Yudhishthira then turned his face to the east and set forth towards the rising-sun. His brothers and Queen Draupadi followed him. As they started, King Yudhishthira's hunting dog joined them, and though the serving men would have driven him away, he refused to leave his master. King Yudhishthira rebuked the serving men, and said, 'The dog comes as a suppliant to my feet. And no Aryan King rejects the prayer of a suppliant. Let the dog, therefore, come with us also.'

In this way King Yudhishthira, his brothers, his Queen, and the King's faithful hound set forth together for Hastinapura upon their last journey.

XVIII

THE REUNION OF THE BHARATAS

WHEN Prince Arjuna set forth with King Yudhishthira, he slung across his shoulders the mighty Gandiva bow and its inexhaustible quiver. For, although his arms, chill with years, had no longer the strength to pull the bowstring, yet the Bharata Prince would not part with the celestial weapon, which in the years gone by had helped him to do such glorious deeds. As the King, his brothers, and their Queen walked towards the rising sun, they saw in front of them a column of golden fire. It came nearer and nearer and rose higher and higher, until it seemed to join together earth and heaven. Then a voice exquisitely clear, yet louder far than that of any mortal man, called to them from the column: 'O Princes of the great Bharata line, I am Agni the fire-god, and I have come to claim from Prince Arjuna the celestial bow which I begged for him in the olden time from Varuna the sea-god. As Arjuna can no longer bend the sea-god's bow, let him take it to the sea-shore and cast it into the ocean. Thus to the sea-god will go back the sea-god's weapon.' King Yudhishthira and his brothers and Queen Draupadi prostrated themselves when they heard the voice of the fire-god. And when they again looked upwards the column of fire had vanished.

Obedient to the fire-god's words, they walked ever towards the rising sun until they came to the shores of the eastern sea, which to-day men call the Bay of Bengal. There Prince Arjuna swung round his head the Gandiva bow and its inexhaustible quiver, and with all his strength threw them far out to sea. Varuna, the sea-god, seized them as they floated, and once again he took the bow in his hand and fitted the quiver upon his mighty shoulders.

PRINCE ARJUNA THROWS THE BOW INTO THE SEA

Leaving the shores of the eastern sea, the Bharata Princes turned westward and walked across all India until they reached the spot near which had once stood Dwarka, the beautiful city of the Yadhavs by the western sea. There, just as it had come to Krishna, a longing came to King Yudhishthira to see the cool white peaks and the pine-clad slopes of the Himalaya Mountains. So he changed again his course, and day by day marched northwards until his eyes rested on the snow-clad ranges that guarded the land of the Aryan Kings. When they had climbed the southern foot-hills, Queen Draupadi grew weary and fell by the way. 'O King,' cried Prince Bhima, 'why has Queen Draupadi left us? Never in her life did she commit a sin. Why, then, has death claimed her before our journey's end?' King Yudhishthira answered without halting: 'Queen Draupadi was the wife of us all, and she should have loved us all equally. But better than all of us she loved Arjuna the archer. That was her sin, and for that she has been punished.'

A few miles farther on Sahadev's knees sank beneath him, and he fell motionless upon the ground. 'O King,' cried Prince Bhima, 'my brother Sahadev, who served thee faithfully all his life, has fallen to earth. He was without sin. Why, therefore, did death claim him before his journey's end?' The King never paused in his march, but answered, 'Sahadev served me faithfully, but in his heart he thought that he was wiser than I—nay, wiser than all men. That was his sin, and for that he has been punished.'

Hardly had King Yudhishthira spoken, when Prince Nakula, the handsomest in face of all the brothers, fell forward and made no effort to raise himself. 'O King,' cried Prince Bhima, 'my brother Nakula, who surpassed us all in beauty of face, has died on the way. He was without sin. Why, then, did death claim him before his journey's end?' The King strode onwards, and without turning his head replied, 'He was in truth a just Prince and worthy in every way of the great Bharata line. But in his heart he thought that his fair face placed him high above all other men. That was his sin, and for that he has been punished.'

The three remaining brothers walked on without speaking for a score of miles. Then the tall and graceful form of Prince Arjuna rolled helplessly in the snow. 'O King,' cried Prince Bhima, 'Arjuna thy brother is dead—Arjuna the greatest archer in all the world. What sin did he, the bravest and kindliest of us all, commit? And why has death claimed him before his journey's end?' King Yudhishthira walked on a few steps in silence. Then he answered, 'Arjuna promised me that he would destroy Duryodhan and his host in a second of time. But he kept not his promise, for it was an idle boast. That was his sin, and for that he has been punished.'

A league farther on Prince Bhima felt his knees grow weak, and for the first time in all his life fear entered his mighty heart. For a few yards he struggled on, then he sank to earth. Looking towards Yudhishthira, he cried, 'O King, I, Bhima, thy last brother, am dying. What sin did I commit that I may not see our journey's end?' The tears coursed down the King's bronzed cheek, for he loved Bhima best of all his brothers. Without turning his head, but with broken voice, he answered, 'Thy strength was great, but thy pride in it was greater still. That was thy sin, and for that thou art punished.'

There remained with King Yudhishthira, out of all his companions, only his faithful hunting dog. With him the King walked slowly onwards until at last he saw in front of him an aerial chariot, in which sat a shining figure with a thousand eyes. King Yudhishthira, because of the thousand eyes, knew the figure to be that of the god Indra. A moment later the god said, 'O Bharata King, thou art weary with walking. Enter my car, and in it I will drive thee swiftly to my celestial city, Amravati.' But the King answered, 'Lord Indra, my brothers have fallen by the wayside. So too has Draupadi my Queen. Unless thou wilt go back with me and take them with thee in thy car, I cannot enter it.' 'O King,' said the god, 'have no care for thy brothers or thy Queen. They have already reached Amravati, my city, before thee.' 'Lord Indra,' said King Yudhishthira, 'I have with me my hunting dog, and he must come with me in the car.' 'O King,' said the god Indra, and his thousand eyes looked scornfully at Yudhishthira, 'I cannot take a dog into my heaven. Leave him, therefore, behind thee and enter my car.' 'Nay, Lord Indra,' said the King, 'this dog came to me as a suppliant when I set out on my journey. I am a Bharata King, and no Bharata King has ever flouted a suppliant. Unless thou permit my hunting dog to enter it with me, I cannot enter thy car.' The god Indra smiled on the King and said, 'King Yudhishthira, I was but testing thy worth, and thou hast fully stood the trial. Enter thou my car and bring thy hound with thee.'

The celestial car bore the god and the King swiftly to Indra's heaven. But when King Yudhishthira entered the golden gates of Amravati, he looked in vain for his brothers and his Queen. 'Lord Indra,' said the King, 'thou hast deceived me. My brothers and my Queen are not in thy heaven. And unless they dwell there with me, I shall not stay in it. I pray thee, therefore, guide me to where they are.' 'As thou wilt, O King,' said the god Indra; 'I will give thee a messenger and he

PRINCE ARJUNA FALLS IN THE SNOW

shall guide thee to thy brothers and thy Queen.'

The messenger led the King back through the golden doors and out of Indra's city. He took a path which gradually grew more and more rugged underfoot. As they walked, the King saw on either hand hideous bushes on which grew human hair, and trees of which the fruits were human bones. And the sky grew darker and darker and the air fouler and fouler, until at last the King could bear the sights and stench no more. He was about to turn back to heaven, when from every side he heard cries, saying, 'Stay, O King, for while thou stayest with us we have ease from our torments.' And the voices which cried to him were the voices of his brothers and of Queen Draupadi. The King called to them, asking them who they were, and the voices replied, saying, 'I am Bhima,' 'I am Arjuna,' 'I am Nakula,' 'I am Sahadev,' 'I am Draupadi.' Then a fierce anger rose in King Yudhishthira's breast, because of the cruel deeds of the gods. He turned to Indra's messenger and said, 'Tell thou the god Indra that if this is his kindness, I will have none of it. Where my brothers and my Queen are there shall I stay. And the torments which they suffer, these I will gladly share with them.'

But as the words left his lips, King Yudhishthira became aware that he stood once more within the golden gates of Indra's city Amravati, and that on every side of him stood a great company of shining figures. The god Indra came nigh to the King. And his thousand eyes smiled on Yudhishthira an infinite welcome. 'Nay, be not angry, O Bharata King,' said Indra, 'this was but another trial by which I tested thee, and once again thou hast borne thyself nobly.' The King looked again at the celestial company. In the front rank he saw coming towards him Bhima the mighty, and Arjuna first of archers, and Sahadev the skilled swordsman, and Nakula the beautiful. Behind them he saw, lovely as in her peerless youth, the face of Draupadi, the dark Princess, whom Arjuna had won on the archery ground of the Panchalas.

Behind his brothers and his Queen he saw all the dead Bharata Princes and the warriors who had fought for or against the Pandava Princes, before they came by their own. There Karna, the sun-god's child, greeted Arjuna his brother and rival. There King Dhritarashtra looked with loving eyes upon the nephews whom in life he had so bitterly hated. There, too, were Bhishma the wise old Prince and Drona the hero, Virata the kindly King, and Drupada, who had called down the curse on the house of the Bharatas. There, too, Yudhishthira saw the burly form of Duryodhana[1] his enemy. But his fine features were no longer marred by the evil thoughts within. And anger passed from Yudhishthira's heart, and love for his cousin took the place of his former hatred. And he greeted him with the same joy as that with which he greeted his brothers.

Thus, freed from the curse of King Drupada and the consequences of their own frailties and sins, the great house of the Bharatas were in Indra's heaven reunited for ever.

1 See Appendix C.

APPENDIX A.—p. 71.

King Krishna of Dwarka.—In the Mahabharata Krishna, King of Dwarka, is a god and not a hero. But as I wished to tell the story of the Bharata Princes only, I have introduced King Krishna more as a hero than as a god. The change, however, has involved a certain amount of reconstruction in the story. I would refer those of my readers who wish to learn about Krishna, the Divine One, to the Bhagwat-Gita, the Shri Madbhagvat, and the Harivansha.

APPENDIX B.—p. 118.

The Death of Bhishma.—In the original text there is some uncertainty as to the time of Bhishma's death. In the beginning of the Drona Parva—that is, in the middle of the battle—Bhishma is spoken of as already dead. But in the Shanti Parva, which describes events after the end of the battle, Bhishma is still alive, and he discourses at immense length on a great variety of topics. I have elected to fix the death of Bhishma as taking place during the battle.

APPENDIX C.—p. 143.

I should note that Duryodhan is not mentioned by name among those whom King Yudhishthira met in Indra's heaven. But I think that he can be included in the phrase addressed by Janamejaya to Vaishampayana, "others whom you have not mentioned." As Drupada was included in the celestial company, there was no reason why Duryodhan should not also have found a place there.